Teaching Embodied

Teaching Embodied

CULTURAL PRACTICE IN JAPANESE PRESCHOOLS

Akiko Hayashi and
Joseph Tobin

The University of Chicago Press
Chicago and London

Akiko Hayashi is a postdoctoral fellow in education at the University of Georgia. **Joseph Tobin** is professor of early childhood education at the University of Georgia and an author or editor of several books, including *Preschool in Three Cultures Revisited*, also published by the University of Chicago Press.

The University of Chicago Press, Chicago 60637
The University of Chicago Press, Ltd., London
© 2015 by The University of Chicago
All rights reserved. Published 2015.
Printed in the United States of America

24 23 22 21 20 19 18 17 16 15   1 2 3 4 5

ISBN-13: 978-0-226-26307-6 (cloth)
ISBN-13: 978-0-226-26310-6 (paper)
ISBN-13: 978-0-226-26324-3 (e-book)

DOI: 10.7208/chicago/9780226263243.001.0001

Library of Congress Cataloging-in-Publication Data
Hayashi, Akiko, 1979– author.
    Teaching embodied : cultural practice in Japanese preschools / Akiko Hayashi and Joseph Tobin.
        pages ; cm
    Includes bibliographical references and index.
    ISBN 978-0-226-26307-6 (cloth : alk. paper) —
ISBN 978-0-226-26310-6 (pbk. : alk. paper) —
ISBN 978-0-226-26324-3 (ebook)   1. Preschool
teachers—Japan. 2. Education, Preschool—
Psychological aspects. 3. Teaching—Psychological
aspects. 4. Child development—Japan.
5. Educational psychology—Japan. 6. Educational
psychology. I. Tobin, Joseph Jay, author. II. Title.
    LB1140.25.J3H39 2015
    372.110952—dc23
                                2015007717

♾ This paper meets the requirements of ANSI/NISO
Z39.48-1992 (Permanence of Paper).

Contents

Preface

This book reflects the fruits of a collaboration between an American anthropologist with over thirty years' experience doing research in Japan and a Japanese psychologist-turned-anthropologist living and working abroad and therefore viewing her own culture with something of an outsider's perspective. It is a synthesis of the interests we brought to the project on children's social-emotional development and preschools as sites that both reflect and reproduce culture.

In this book we present analyses of young children's interactions in preschools, but most of our attention is on their teachers. We suggest that across a variety of types of Japanese preschools, teachers share some core implicit cultural beliefs and practices. While this study focuses on teachers and children in Japanese preschools, we believe that the methods and conceptual framework we have employed in this study and our central findings have implications for teaching and learning in other countries as well.

Our title, "Teaching Embodied," can be read in different ways, including "teaching made visible and tangible," "teaching exemplified," "the essence of teaching," and "teaching as embodied practice." Throughout this book we use the concept of "embodied practice" in two ways: One is the teacher's use of her body as a pedagogical tool, how she uses her gaze, touch, posture, and location in the classroom. The other refers to aspects of professional practice that seem to the teachers we interviewed to result more from "muscle memory," tacit knowledge, and intuitive action than from conscious intention. We document how the three Japanese preschool teachers who are the focus of our study use embodied practices to support young children's social-emotional development and how their students learn to use their bodies in culturally normative ways to negotiate social relations in preschool classrooms. We present analyses not only of how these teachers act, but also of how they think and talk about their actions.

A focus on embodied aspects of teaching and learning calls for a method of conducting research and a mode of description and analysis that combine words and images. Therefore this is a visually rich book. The text has over two hundred illustrations, still images we "grabbed" from the videos we made of daily life in Japanese preschool classrooms that served as the raw data for this study. We believe that a great strength of this project is the integration of pictures and words, of images of Japanese preschool educators and children combined with their words, and ours. Through such an integration of word and image it is possible to get closer to appreciating the wholeness of life in Japanese preschools, and elsewhere.

Neither of us could have done this project without the other. We have worked collaboratively on each step of the research process, from shooting and editing the videos, to conducting interviews with teachers and directors, to analyzing interview transcripts and video clips, to writing the manuscript.

The teachers and directors of the preschools where we conducted our fieldwork and interviews gave us the key ideas for this study. We treasure our ongoing professional relationships with the teachers and directors at Komatsudani Hoikuen, Madoka Yōchien, Meisei Gakuen, and Senzan Yōchien. Thank you all for not only helping us but also believing in us. We will repay your trust by continuing to conduct our research sincerely.

Akiko Hayashi and Joe Tobin
Tokyo, Japan, and Athens, Georgia, 2014

Introduction

In a daycare classroom in Kyoto, four little girls fight for possession of a teddy bear, with a tussle on the floor and tears, while their teacher looks on, at one point calling out, "Hey," but otherwise not intervening. In a kindergarten in Tokyo a four-year-old boy pulls another boy's hair, and their teacher spends ten minutes squatting down between the boys, mediating their dispute, while other children gather around to look and listen. On the playground of a school for the deaf in Tokyo, several four-year-olds argue (in Japanese Sign Language) about the fairness of the two sides that have formed for a tug of war, while their teacher looks on, not attempting to mediate even when their disagreement becomes heated and includes grabbing and shoving. These and other incidents we analyze in this book reflect the interactions of children's and teachers' bodies, intentions, and words; of customs, habits, and beliefs; of affordances provided by the architecture and materiality of the Japanese preschool classroom and playground; of organizational and economic features of Japanese preschools, including government-mandated student/teacher ratios, curriculum guidelines, and teacher career trajectories; and of such elements of happenstance as a rainstorm that moves recess indoors and the absence of a sick child who might otherwise have played a mediating role in a dispute.

At its core, this is a study of how Japanese preschool teachers act, think, and talk. More specifically, it is a study of the practices they use to support young children's social-emotional development. Our study is centered on the everyday professional practices, recorded on video, of three Japanese preschool teachers working in three Japanese early childhood contexts. At the time the videos were shot in their classrooms, these three teachers were about the same age (late twenties) with similar levels of experience (about three years). Chisato Morita teaches at Komatsudani Hoikuen (daycare center) in Kyoto, a full-day program supported with public funds, for children of working parents, located in a Buddhist temple in Kyoto and led by a Buddhist priest. Mariko Kaizuka teaches at Madoka Yōchien in Tokyo, a private kindergarten, run as a family business, offering a part-day program, in a

Figure 0.1. Chisato Morita.

Figure 0.2. Mariko Kaizuka.

Figure 0.3. Akiko Ikeda.

bustling urban neighborhood. Akiko Ikeda, the third teacher we feature in this study, is the lead teacher of the preschool class at Meisei Gakuen, a private school for the deaf in Tokyo, run as a nonprofit organization, dedicated to offering parents and children the option, elsewhere unavailable in Japan, of a sign language education in a setting that features Deaf culture.

Two of the three preschools we feature in this study were research sites for *Preschool in Three Cultures Revisited*: Komatsudani Hoikuen and Madoka Yōchien. The third school, Meisei Gakuen, is one of the research sites for the Deaf Kindergarten in Three Countries study, for which we are members of the research team. In this book, however, our focus is not on Deaf education, but instead on Meisei as a Japanese preschool, and on Akiko Ikeda as a Japanese teacher. We do not ignore the theme of deafness, but we view the deafness of the children and teachers at Meisei as a variation on Japanese preschool pedagogy.

As in the Preschool in Three Cultures studies (Tobin, Wu, and Davidson 1989; Tobin, Hsueh, and Karasawa 2009), we use videos filmed in each teacher's classroom as interviewing cues; but unlike those studies, this study also uses the videos as data, presenting microanalyses of key scenes. In this book, as in those studies, we attend to teachers' verbal reflections on their practice, but also to teachers' techniques of the body, which we suggest are key components of their practice.

ON CULTURAL EXPLANATIONS

Throughout this book we provide cultural explanations of teaching, but we strive to do so in a way that avoids reductionist versions of culture. We are aware of the danger of reifying the concept of culture and producing tautological analyses that amount to an argument that "the Japanese teach the way they do because they are Japanese" (Anderson-Levitt 2012). To suggest that a practice is cultural does not mean that it is not also informed and shaped by policy, the affordances and constraints of the classroom environment, and economic and demographic factors. We find useful Anderson-Levitt's definition of the cultural dimensions of teaching as "traces of prior processes of meaning making" that "afford and constrain what will happen in new social situations" (Anderson-Levitt 2013, 6). This definition has the virtue of conceptualizing culture as having an impact on without solely determining teaching practices. As Anderson-Levitt argues, while culture affords and constrains how people will behave in a new situation, "it is still the people in those new situations who have to make meanings anew, using those traces, those artifacts as resources" (6). What Anderson-Levitt calls "artifacts," "resources," and "traces," we call "implicit cultural practices."

We define implicit cultural practices as practices that have three core characteristics. First, rather than being idiosyncratic, these practices are largely (but not universally) shared among members of a profession in a country or region. Second, while not unconscious or repressed, they are seldom talked about or consciously thought about (at least not until such talk and thought are provoked by researchers). And third, they rarely are mentioned in government guidelines, curriculum standards, or teacher education textbooks. In this book we provide examples of Japanese preschool teachers dealing with a range of classroom situations, some familiar, some novel, by drawing on a repertoire of cultural beliefs and practices, explicit, implicit, and tacit.

We believe in the power and utility of culture as an explanatory tool for studying life in schools, but not of just any notion of culture. We bring to our analysis of Japanese preschool pedagogy an approach that sees culture as not only conscious and explicit, but also tacit; not only mediated by words, but also nonlinguistic; not only cognitive, but also embodied; and not only individual and internal, but also collective and intercorporeal.

BODIES AND MINDS

In a 1934 essay, Marcel Mauss suggested that techniques of the body, rather than being idiosyncratic, are characteristic of an era, culture, social class, or occupational group, and are things people do without the need for planning, intent, or reflection. Mauss (1934/1973) argued that people sit, walk, run, swim, dance, and converse in ways that are characteristic of their culture, gender, and social class, although these bodily practices are not systematically taught, prescribed, or available to conscious intent.

The argument of this book, following Mauss, is that much of what Japanese preschool teachers do in their classrooms, including the ways they deal with children's fights, involves the use of techniques of the body whose functioning teachers sometimes find difficult to explain. While much about preschool teaching in Japan, as in other countries, is intentional and explicit, in the sense of prescribed by ministry guidelines, taught in schools of education, reinforced by administrators, discussed in teacher workshops, and written down in curriculum plans, many of the most salient of Japanese preschool practices are the result more of habitus, intuition, and emergence than of policy, orthodoxy, or plan. We can gain a deeper understanding of early childhood education in Japan (and elsewhere) if we pay more attention to implicit and especially to embodied dimensions of professional practice and to emergent rather than only to planned and intended aspects of classroom events.

In arguing for the importance of attending to teachers' bodily techniques, our intent is not to oppose the body to the mind. By identifying some teaching practices as techniques of the body we do not mean to suggest that the mind is not also involved. In postgame interviews athletes sometimes use the phrases "body memory" and "muscle memory" to explain something they did in the heat of action, without seeming to have had the time for calculation and planning. But it would be nonsensical to suggest that muscles acting alone, without the involvement of the mind, can do something as complex as hit, throw, or kick a ball with a certain speed and trajectory, to achieve a desired outcome. Such skilled bodily actions of proficient athletes require an integration of mind and body. Our argument is that the same is true for the practices of accomplished Japanese preschool teachers.

In his essay on the status of the body in sociological theory, Nick Crossley (2007) uses typing as an example of an embodied activity that requires the acquisition of a set of skills, but that does not require conscious attention:

> Typing, for example, involves movement of my fingers, arms, eyes, head etc. This is purposive, intelligent and cultured movement. . . . My fingers know where to go without me having to look or search but I couldn't discursively describe where individual letters are. My knowledge of the keyboard is practical, pre-reflective and embodied. And from the point of view of my consciousness, my body "just moves" appropriately, without my interference. . . . From the point of view of consciousness, culturally appropriate bodily action and coordination "just happens" and falls below the threshold of perception and reflective knowledge. (83)

We will demonstrate in the chapters that follow that this is much the way experienced Japanese preschool teachers react to requests to explain the thinking behind their embodied practices. In our interviews, teachers told us they rarely think about how they position themselves in the classroom, the postures they assume while reading a story or mediating a dispute, or the facial expressions and tone of voice they employ when talking with children about an emotional event. Many of their actions fall below the threshold of conscious attention. This is not to say that teachers have nothing interesting to say about their practice. When pressed for explanations of their actions (as informants routinely are in ethnographic studies), teachers can and do present interesting reflections. But rather than assume that these post hoc reflections are the intentions or underlying causes that produced the practices captured in our videos, we instead view teachers' talk about their practice as another form of implicit cultural and professional practice. Talk, after all, is no less reflective of culture and profession than are techniques of the body.

Most accounts of teaching assume that good practice begins with a conscious intent in the teacher's mind that the teacher then operationalizes, first with a lesson plan, and then by instructing her body to carry out this plan. We draw on a range of theorists to turn this model on its head and suggest that action, including the practice of preschool teaching, sometimes or perhaps even usually comes before rather than after intention. Louis Althusser (1971), citing an example from Blaise Pascal, suggests that you are religious because you pray, in contrast to the conventional reasoning that you pray because you are religious. The material, embodied practices of religion (for Catholics, kneeling down, making the sign of the cross, taking communion) precede and construct the religious ideation. The bodily practice comes first and the belief follows. Such, we suggest, is the case for much about preschool teaching in Japan (and elsewhere).

Pierre Bourdieu (2000) critiques the "scholastic blindness" that leads scholars to privilege the mind above the body and theory over practical knowledge. He criticizes rational actor models of behavior and the idea of "voluntary deliberation," an idea that assumes that

> Every decision, conceived as a theoretical choice among theoretical possibles constituted as such, presupposes two preliminary operations: first, drawing up a complete list of possible choices; secondly, determining the consequences of the different strategies and evaluating them comparatively. This totally unrealistic representation of ordinary action. . . . is based on the idea that every action is preceded by a premeditated and explicit plan. (137–38)

Such notions of rational action, premeditation, and deliberation are characteristic of most scholarship on teaching and most programs of teacher education, which give more emphasis to the writing of lesson plans than to spontaneous decision making and more attention to teacher post hoc reflection than to their embodied, intuitive practice. Bourdieu's argument can be used to shift our attention from teaching as premeditated action to teaching as embodied, emergent practice. Bourdieu opposes rational action theories with the concept of *habitus*:

> Social agents are endowed with *habitus*, inscribed in their bodies by past experiences. These systems of schemes of perception, apprecia-tion and action enable them to perform acts of practical knowledge, based on the identification and recognition of conditional, conven-tional stimuli to which they are predisposed to react; and, without any explicit definition of ends or rational calculation of means, to gener-ate appropriate and endlessly renewed strategies, but within the limits of the structural constraints of which they are the product and which define them. (138)

In sum, we are concerned with two meanings of embodiment. One is a teacher's literal use of her body as a tool, how she uses her hands to gesture, comfort, and discipline; her posture, gaze, and location in the classroom to indicate varying levels of attention; her voice to communicate empathy, frus-tration, disapproval, and enthusiasm. A second, related meaning is teaching practices that lack premeditation and reflection and rely on "muscle mem-ory" analogous to that of athletes and musicians.

TACIT AND IMPLICIT KNOWLEDGE

Michael Polanyi argues that in science and medicine, as in other domains of everyday life, much of the knowledge that guides us is tacit. His position is summarized in his dictum: "There are things that we know but cannot tell" (Polanyi 1962, 601). Polanyi makes a useful distinction between a complex practice, such as playing a piece of music on the piano, and the component parts of the practice, which include the spacing of the fingers, the posture of the body, the use of the foot pedals, and the order and combination in which keys are struck to produce notes and chords. Each of the components can be practiced separately, but, Polanyi argues, if an accomplished concert pia-nist focuses too much attention on the parts, he or she will lose the fluidity that turns mere piano playing into virtuoso performance that communicates deep feeling and beauty.

The anthropologist Maurice Bloch (1991) arrives at a similar conclusion, as he argues that because "much of the knowledge which anthropologists study necessarily exists in people's heads in a non-linguistic form," we should be suspicious of the language-based explanations of practices that we anthropologists provoke our informants to provide:

> When our informants honestly say "This is why we do such things," or "This is what this means," or "This is how we do such things," instead of being pleased we should be suspicious and ask what kind of peculiar knowledge is this which can take such an explicit, linguistic form? Indeed, we should treat all explicit knowledge as problematic, as a type of knowledge probably remote from that employed in practical activities under normal circumstances. (193–94)

Max van Manen's (1995) concept of "pedagogical tact" suggests similarly that teaching expertise is not organized in the form of language:

> This practical skill is like a silent knowledge that is implicit in my world and in my actions rather than cognitively explicit or critically reflective. This silent knowledge cannot necessarily be translated back into propositional discourse. . . . Good teachers often have difficulty identifying why things work so well for them (or why they do not work well for that matter). If teachers are requested to account for their successes or if they are asked to convert their actions into verbal propositions then they will normally be tempted to reproduce the kinds of abstracted principles or theories that they feel are expected of them. What else can they do? It is much more difficult to capture in language the kind of knowledge that inheres in our body and in the things of our world. (10–12)

We are interested in Japanese preschool teachers' explanations for why and how they do things and in the meanings they attach to their practices. But we take from Bloch, Polanyi, and van Manen an awareness that we should not mistake such verbal discourses about practice for underlying causes, or get so caught up in informants' words about practice that we fail to document, present, and analyze the embodied practices themselves. A provocative implication of Bloch's theory of nonlinguistic knowledge and Polanyi's of the tacit knowledge of expert practitioners is that translating embodied practices into linguistic form is counterproductive, as it introduces a self-consciousness that may interfere with fluidity.

The terms tacit and implicit are often used interchangeably in discussions of professional practice. While we see the concepts covered by these terms as overlapping, we make a distinction: we use the term "implicit" for the pedagogical practices that, although not written down in guidelines or textbooks or talked about by teachers in their daily lives, teachers can explain relatively easily when pushed to do so by ethnographers. We use the term "tacit" to refer to the embodied techniques practitioners employ to perform these implicit pedagogical practices, techniques difficult for most practitioners to explain even when pushed by ethnographers to do so. For example, in chapter 1 we suggest that *mimamoru*, which we define as a low-intervention approach to dealing with children's struggles, is a common pedagogical strategy that is implicit; in contrast, we use the terms "tacit," "techniques of the body," and "bodily habitus" to refer to the ways teachers modulate their location in the classroom and especially their performance of attention and inattention to let children know they are aware of what is going on but are not about to intervene.

EXPERTISE

We are interested not only in identifying core characteristics of Japanese preschool teaching, but also in distinguishing between teaching and teaching well, and in identifying the processes that contribute to the development of teaching expertise. Our interviews with teachers and directors suggest that the most culturally characteristic of Japanese preschool teaching practices are learned on the job, through experience, rather than in teacher education programs or in in-service professional development sessions. This is particularly true for those pedagogical practices that are most clearly techniques of the body, such as facial expressions, posture, gaze, and location in the classroom. These aspects of teaching are challenging to teach to beginning teachers because they are nonlinguistic and in most cases below the threshold of conscious attention or reflection. As Jane White (1989) writes in her analysis of student teaching in the United States:

Some of the cultural knowledge of teaching is nonverbal. Much of the knowledge acquired at the very beginning of student teaching is physical and imitative—eye gaze, posture, pitch of voice, intonation, and has to do with how to talk as a teacher. Much of what is learned has to do with space and time: learning where to stand, learning how to pace and sequence questions, learning what to do when a child gives a wrong answer. (193)

Van Manen (1995), building on a concept first developed by Johann Herbart, uses the term "pedagogical thoughtfulness and tact" to describe the way expert teachers employ "the improvisational pedagogical-didactical skill of instantly knowing, from moment to moment, how to deal with students in interactive teaching-learning situations" (8). We draw as well on David Berliner's (1988) suggestion that as teachers gain experience, they become increasingly "arational" (which is not the same thing as nonrational). They become less driven by rules, less consciously deliberative, and more confident in following their intuition.

CONTINGENCY AND EMERGENCE

To call a teaching practice an implicit cultural practice or an embodied form of habitus does not mean it is unchanging or unresponsive to new situations. As Bourdieu (2000) writes: "Habitus change constantly in response to new experiences. Dispositions are subject to a kind of permanent revision" (161). We apply this logic at various points in this book to explain, for example, the network of bodies, things, habitus, beliefs, and structural constraints and affordances that are in play when a group of girls at Komatsudani Hoikuen fight over a teddy bear and Morita does not intervene other than at one point to call out "Hey!" from across the room. When reflecting on this scene in our video, Morita explained to us that she sometimes intervenes in children's fights, and sometimes does not, and that the decision depends on many factors. When we asked Morita how she handles children's fights, she replied: "Sono toki ni yōtte" (It depends). In the case of the teddy bear fight, Morita explained that her actions depended on a variety of factors, including that when the fight broke out she was busy cleaning up the classroom before lunch, and that at one point in the fight the girls were in close proximity to the sharp edge of a piano.

Contingency and emergence occur in all domains, but are particularly characteristic of domains that are, in Rand Spiro's term, "ill-structured."

Spiro and his colleagues Feltovich, Jacobsen, and Coulson (1992) define an ill-structured domain as one in which practitioners must deal with cases of which no two are exactly alike and that involve the interaction of multiple factors. They list as examples of ill-structured domains medicine, history, and literary interpretation. We would add to this list preschool teaching, which is perhaps the most ill-structured, in Spiro's sense, of all levels of education. This is particularly the case in Japan, where the national kindergarten guidelines provide only general goals and teaching is not dominated by standardized curricula or driven by standardized assessment of children or teachers.

Spiro, Collins, and Ramchandran (2007) write: "In complex and more ill-structured arenas of knowledge," approaches are needed "that foster the building of knowledge characterized by multiple representation, interconnectedness, and contingency (context-dependence, a tendency to recognize when it is appropriate to say 'it depends' and to acknowledge that many situations are not 'either/or,' but rather shades of gray in between" (20). They argue that ill-structured domains require practitioners to employ "complex, open, and flexible habits of mind" (19). We extend this concept by arguing that certain ill-structured domains such as preschool teaching demand complex, open, and flexible habits of the *body*. Preschool teaching is less like a sport such as high jumping in which the challenge and therefore the required bodily technique are always much the same and more like a sport such as soccer that has few fixed plays and demands of its expert practitioners the ability to combine, on the fly, a repertoire of embodied skills to cope with constantly changing situations, no two of which are precisely alike.

INTERCORPOREALITY

No matter how skillfully teachers employ bodily techniques in their classrooms, their pedagogy can be effective only if their actions are reciprocated by those of their students. Teaching is not a solo performance but a group production, requiring the harmonization of movements of a teacher and her students. As in a dance ensemble, or a soccer team, preschool students and their teacher must coordinate their bodily practices. But unlike a dance company or a sports team, a preschool classroom is not directed to accomplishing a single shared goal. For this reason, we suggest another useful metaphor is the way commuters navigate crowded subway stations and city streets, employing techniques of the body, mostly unconsciously, to avoid collisions on their way to their separate destinations. For their first few months in the city, newcomers to urban life are likely to be jostled and to jostle others in the station, to clumsily board and leave train cars, and to struggle to know where exactly to stand on a crowded train and which strap or pole to grab. Similar awkwardness characterizes students' movements in the first few months of the school year and teachers' movements in their first few years on the job. Erving Goffman coined the phrase "the spatiality of embodiment" to describe the synchronization of bodies that social life requires, a form of sociality Maurice Merleau-Ponty conceptualizes as "intercorporeality" (Crossley 1995).

For life in the classroom to flow, there must be a synchronicity, a harmony of movement of experienced teachers with a class of children who are in the process of assimilating the bodily techniques of their classroom society. Teachers therefore have a twofold task: they must master techniques of using their own body as a pedagogical tool, and also learn how to support the development in children of embodied, intercorporeal social practices. The Japanese *Kindergarten Education Guidelines* states that a key curriculum goal is the development in children of social mindedness and group-living skills (*shakai seikatsu*). Our focus is on how Japanese preschool teachers help young children learn to attune their bodies to group life. To live appropriately in Japanese society requires the mastery not just of one way of being in the world, but of several, and of the ability to modulate one's behavior and bodily practices according to shifting contextual demands. In Japanese preschools there are several moments each day when teachers lead children in shifting their language and bodily demeanor from informal to formal registers.

SOCIAL-EMOTIONAL DEVELOPMENT AND SOCIAL MINDEDNESS

Our study is centered on the role Japanese preschool educators play in young children's social-emotional development and in the development of what Japanese early childhood educators call "social mindedness" (*shakai seikatsu*). We have chosen this emphasis for several reasons. One is that there is widespread agreement among Japanese policymakers, teachers, and parents that the most important function of the Japanese preschool is to support children's learning to function as members of society. While there are some preschools in Japan that emphasize academic preparation (Holloway 2000), they are clearly in the minority (Oda and Mori 2006).

Our focus also reflects our ethnographic orientation. A central concern of ethnography is enculturation, the processes through which culture is transmitted from one generation to the next. A central goal of enculturation in Japan, as elsewhere, is helping children learn to be appropriate members of society. To function as a member of a social group in any culture requires developing social skills, including the ability both to display emotions appropriately and to respond appropriately to the emotions of others. Research has shown that while there are some aspects of emotionality that are much the same across cultures (Eisenberg 1992), there are also culturally characteristic ways of feeling, showing one's feelings, and responding to the feelings of others (Lebra 1976; Markus and Kitayama 1991).

Japanese preschool teachers sometimes commented in our interviews on the emotional characteristics and social abilities of the individual children in their class, but they gave greater emphasis to the progress they saw over time in the collective ability of their class to handle social interactions. We suggest that Japanese early childhood educators' discussions of social mindedness differ from most Western conceptions of social-emotional development by viewing children's capacity to handle disputes and other social interactions as a function more of the class as a community than of each child as an individual. A Japanese view of social-emotional development can push us to consider how impulse control and other aspects of what developmental psychologists call "executive functions" can be seen as characteristics not just or primarily of individual preschool children, but also of the collective capacity of a classroom.

Another way to describe our central research question is: How do Japanese preschools function as sites where Japanese children learn to be Japanese? However, when we asked our informants how they think about this question, they told us that they rarely if ever think of what they are doing in preschool as teaching their students to relate to each other in Japanese ways. They told us that their intention is to teach young children how to be happy, well-adjusted members of the classroom community, not to make them Japanese. They do this occasionally with didactic instruction, but mostly by modeling and by providing opportunities for social interaction and for children to experience a range of emotions. It is up to outsiders like us to notice in what ways the version of being happy and well-adjusted that is taught and learned in Japanese preschools is particularly Japanese.

OUR RESEARCH METHODS

If much of preschool practice is below the threshold of teachers' perception and reflective knowledge and takes the form of knowledge that, as Bloch (1991) and Polanyi (1962; 1966) argue, is fundamentally nonlinguistic and tacit, how can we researchers become aware of such practices and how in turn can we describe and analyze them? In this book we employ two strategies. One is an ethnographic fieldwork method, in which we use our cultural outsiderness to the world of Japanese preschools to provoke cultural insiders to become self-consciously aware of practices that otherwise would remain implicit, tacit, and nonverbalized. The challenge for our informants and for us is to find ways of turning their usually implicit, nonverbally coded, tacit practices into words. The other strategy we employ is to document their practices not only in words, but also in images. In this book we present analyses of the comments made by our informants about the videos we showed them, and also microanalyses of teacher-student interactions in segments from the videos.

The strategies we use here extend and modify the methods used in the Preschool in Three Cultures studies. The method of those studies is video-cued multivocal ethnography. The research teams made twenty-minute videos showing typical days in preschools in Japan, China, and the United States and then used these videos as cues for interviewing (figure 0.4). The first interviews were with the teachers in whose classrooms the videos were made. In these interviews, teachers were asked to explain the thinking behind the practices seen in the videos. To determine the typicality and range of variation of these pedagogical practices, the next step in the method was to conduct interviews with other teachers and administrators at that school, then with educators at other schools in the same country, and then with educators in the other two countries in the study.

In this study our approach differs from that of the Preschool in Three Cultures studies in being more narrowly focused (on one country rather than three and on teachers' views of social-emotional development rather than on the full range of their practices); in employing more in-depth, repeat

Figure 0.4. Ikeda, Tobin, Hayashi, and sign-language interpreter Wakabayashi watch and discuss the Meisei video.

interviews with a core group of teachers and directors; in asking teachers to respond not to the twenty-minute videos as a whole, but instead to selected scenes; and in using the videos not only as interviewing cues but also as data for microanalysis.

The Preschool in Three Cultures studies emphasized that the videos were not data, but rather interviewing cues. The focus of those studies was less on the behaviors captured in the videos than on the teachers' explanations of these practices. In this book we still focus on Japanese educators' reflections on scenes in videos of days in Japanese preschools. But instead of arguing that the images in the videos are cues and not data, we treat them both as cues for interviewing and as data. We will demonstrate that there is much to be learned from microanalyses and close readings of the embodied practices captured in the videos. There is a rich tradition both in ethnography and in video-based studies of teaching of doing close analyses of just a few or even of just a single cultural practitioner. An excellent example is Connor, Asch, and Asch's (1986) video-cued study of a Balinese shaman, a study that was a major influence on the development of the Preschool in Three Cultures method.

We began this project by reanalyzing the transcripts from the interviews with Japanese early childhood educators conducted for *Preschool in Three Cultures Revisited*, (2009), looking for insights that had been overlooked and for reflections by practitioners that focus on how they support children's learning of *shūdan seikatsu* (social life). We next reinterviewed some of the informants who had participated in the earlier study, asking them again to watch and comment on the videos. A third strategy was to re-edit the videos. We went back to the uncut footage, selecting shots that weren't used in the original studies, and we then used these re-edited videos to narrow and in some cases shift the focus of the interviews and to introduce new topics for discussion. Our final strategy was to do careful shot-by-shot analyses of segments of the videos and develop working interpretations, which we then asked our informants to comment on.

A refocusing of the videos required both a conceptual and a literal shifting of focus (Hayashi and Tobin 2012). We went back to the footage that did not make it into the twenty-minute videos and found shots that would provoke discussion of the key issues of this book. To compose each video, fourteen hours of video shot over the course of a single day with two cameras had been reduced to twenty minutes, less than 3 percent of the footage making it into the final version. For example, the fight scene at Madoka included in the video had been reduced from eighteen minutes of uncut tape to three minutes. That meant that we had available fifteen minutes of original footage of this scene that we could salvage from the cutting room floor to make new versions of the video.

Another technique we employed was to use tools in our editing software literally to reframe scenes. The software allowed us to shift the center of shots, moving what had been in the center to one side of the frame and what had been on one side of the frame to the center. Freezing an image, recentering, and zooming, and then again recentering (figure 0.5a and b) is a technique made popular in spy and police procedurals going back to Michelangelo Antonioni's *Blow-Up*, a film that showed how something caught by a camera on the periphery could, with refocusing and enlarging, become the core, the crucial clue. Using editing software, we were able to freeze one shot in the middle of the movie, zoom into a detail that might have been missed, and recenter. Microanalysis of video images allowed us to add to our ethnographic focus on teachers' emic beliefs attention to children's and teachers' bodily techniques and to the intercorporeal nature of classroom life.

In the new study, by using the reedited videos as interviewing cues and by adding repeat interviews with the same informants over time, we were able to go deeper into key pedagogical issues. We found that as our informants got used to being interviewed by us and accustomed to our video-cued method, they took more initiative and their engagement in the project grew. To understand expertise, we needed to see the same teacher at different points in her career. To explore how teachers change over time, we conducted repeat interviews with Chisato Morita of Komatsudani Hoikuen and Mariko Kaizuka of Madoka, whom we first interviewed in 2002, in the third years of their careers. We also reinterviewed some of the other informants

Figure 0.5a and b. Freezing an image, zooming, and recentering.

from the *Preschool in Three Cultures Revisited* study, and asked them again to watch and comment on the videos. We have been in dialogue with some of them from 2002 until now, such as Director Ritsuko Kumagai of Senzan Yōchien in Kyoto, whom we have interviewed seven times, each time returning with new scenes to show her and new questions to ask.

ORGANIZATION OF THE BOOK

There are six thematic chapters, each dealing with an aspect of how Japanese teachers think, act, and talk about the role they play in children's social-emotional development. The focus of chapter 1 is *mimamoru*, a term that literally means "watching and guarding" and that we suggest is an emic pedagogical concept that underlies the low-intervention approach in children's disputes we see teachers employing in each of the videos. Chapter 2 is focused on feelings and on the centrality in preschool pedagogy of the Japanese emic concepts of *omoiyari* (empathy) and *amae* (dependence) and of the value placed on the embodied experience of emotion, including being hurt, physically as well as emotionally. Chapter 3 is concerned with children's peripheral participation in disputes and with an emic pedagogical belief in the value of the *gyarari* (gallery) of children who participate on the periphery of disputes, and in this way not only have a vicarious experience of interpersonal conflict, but also act to mediate the dispute by creating an awareness among the fighters of the presence of "the eyes of society." Chapter 4 is focused on how teachers help children learn to modulate their language, posture, hand gestures, and head position to indicate a shift from informal to formal contexts and back. Chapter 5, which is on the development of pedagogical expertise, focuses on how the three featured teachers in our study reflect on their own development over time as teachers. Chapter 6 is different from the others as we switch from an analysis of preschool pedagogy to an analysis of the emic dimensions of the role of government guidelines. We argue that the guidelines' lack of explicit direction to teachers on questions of pedagogy is itself a form of *mimamoru*—of minimal intervention, that gives the teachers latitude to explore their own best practices. In the concluding chapter we show how the practices we analyzed separately in the preceding chapters are simultaneously present in real life in preschool. We do this by presenting an analysis of a scene of an older child feeding a baby at Komatsudani and a reanalysis of the teddy bear fight that focuses on the interaction of feelings, *mimamoru*, the *gyarari*, touch, policy, and expertise.

Chapter 1

—

Mimamoru (Teaching by Watching and Waiting)

Figure 1.1.

THE TEDDY BEAR FIGHT

An argument breaks out among four girls during free-play time. Nao, Seiko, and Reiko are pulling and tugging on a teddy bear, as Maki stands nearby watching their argument:

> SEIKO: Pull it this way.
> MAKI: Let go!
> SEIKO AND REIKO: We got it! We got it!
> REIKO: She is taking it back!
> SEIKO: We got it. We got it!

The three girls fall to the floor in a pile of twisting, pushing, and pulling bodies. Morita calls from across the room: "Kora, kora" (Hey!), but she doesn't approach the fighting girls. As Nao begins to cry, Reiko says to her: "Nao-chan, it's not yours. It's Seiko's." As Nao continues crying, Seiko, Reiko, Maki, and Yoko discuss what to do. Maki suggests that Seiko should give the bear to Nao. Nao, in tears, comes near to Seiko, who is holding the teddy bear close to her chest.

> SEIKO: Don't cry.
> MAKI: Seiko, give it to her.
> SEIKO: It's okay if you say, "Let me borrow it."
> NAO: Give it to me!
> YOKO: No!
> REIKO: Stop it!
> NAO: Give it to me.
> YOKO: You shouldn't take it.
> REIKO (to YOKO): You should scold her.
> YOKO: That's bad! You can't grab the bear away like that!
> NAO: But I had it first.
> MAKI: But then you put it down, so your turn was over.

Nao is led away to the other side of the room by Seiko, who links little fingers with Nao, the two girls swinging their hands as they sing, "Keep this promise or swallow a thousand needles!" Seiko then says to Nao, "Understand?" and as Nao nods in reply, Seiko puts her arm around Nao's shoulders and the girls walk off together.

MIMAMORU: THE LOGIC OF WATCHING AND WAITING

After showing the teddy bear fight scene to Japanese preschool teachers and directors, we asked them, "What do you think about this scene?" and "What would you do if you were in this situation?" One Japanese teacher explained to us:

> Japanese teachers wait until children solve their problems on their own. Children know what they are capable of handling. So, we wait. You could say that it is because we believe in children that we can wait. Otherwise, children become people who can't do things without permission. Of course, if they are in a situation where they don't know what to do, we talk it over with them, and then we wait and watch [*mimamoru*] to see what happens.

Mimamoru can be defined as "watching over," as in the song lyric, "someone to watch over me." *Mi* means to watch and *mamoru* means to protect. When put together, these two words make a phrase that has two meanings. One is to watch someone carefully in order to keep him or her from harm. The second is to observe and reflect on someone's behavior. For example, *mimamoru* is used in such phrases as "kodomo no seichyō o mimamoru" (to track children's growing) and "nariyuki o mimamoru" (to follow the development of events). A related term used by Japanese educators is *machi no hoiku*. *Hoiku* means nurturing or childrearing. *Machi* is a form of the verb "to wait." *Machi no hoiku* is a pedagogical approach based on waiting, patience, taking a long perspective, and watching rather than acting.

We find examples of this strategy of watching and holding back in Japanese teachers' explanations for a range of pedagogical practices and developmental goals, including giving children opportunities to develop emotional, social, and intellectual skills. As a preschool teacher in Tokyo told us: "We think it's important to support children's emotional development. In order for this to happen, children need time to struggle by themselves. So, we watch over them [*mimamoru*]."

GUARDING

One of the meanings of *mimamoru* is to stand guard. The guard does her job not only or primarily by occasionally intervening, but also by letting people know that someone is on guard. In preschool classrooms, knowing that their teacher is watching over them gives the children the confidence and security they need to try to work things out on their own. She provides a sort of safety net or support for the children's social interaction.

In our interviews, Japanese teachers often used the terms *mimamorareru* (to be watched) and *mimamorareteiru* (to be watched over) in such sentences as "Children need to know that they are being watched by their teacher," and "Being watched gives children confidence." These comments suggest a connection between *mimamoru* and the traditional Japanese concept of *seken no me*. *Seken* literally means "society"; *me* means "eyes." Together they mean literally "the eyes of society." When used outside of school settings, this concept sometimes has a negative meaning, as in suggestions that one is surrounded by nosey neighbors; but usually the phrase is used to refer to

Figure 1.2. Samata-sensei tells Maki to take care.

the positive role of social concern, especially in caring for children. Ethnographic descriptions of Japan in the pre–World War II era describe a culture in which in both rural villages and urban neighborhoods everyone knew each other and everyone took responsibility for watching and, when necessary, correcting children (Embree 1939; Benedict 1946; Smith and Wiswell 1982; Lebra 1976). If a child did something naughty or dangerous on the street, any adult who saw him would let him know he was being watched and that what he was doing was wrong. A lament often heard in contemporary Japan is that this sense of being watched and therefore protected and cared for by the eyes of the community has been lost with urbanization and the decline of traditional neighborhoods and villages. In contemporary Japan, preschool has come to replace the rural village and urban neighborhood as the key site where children can experience the feeling of being watched over.

There is a scene in the Komatsudani video that shows children from the five-year-old class spending time in the infant and toddler rooms and helping care for the younger children. These *tōban* (daily monitors) help the little ones change clothes, eat, play, and even use the bathroom. When we asked, "Isn't this practice dangerous?" Nogami, the teacher of the five-year-old class, answered: "We keep a close watch over [*mimamoru*] the children." In another scene in the Komatsudani video, after the official day is over, we see children playing on the playground and four-year-old Maki is standing on top of a horizontal bar, nearly two meters off the ground. Samata-sensei, standing nearby, says, "Be careful," but she does not stop the girl from continuing her potentially dangerous play. Her watching and waiting here communicates both concern and confidence (figure 1.2).

The central point here is not that teachers in Japanese preschools hesitate to intervene, but that while not intervening they let the children know that they are aware of what is going on. This is a complex dynamic. On the one hand, when children are doing something potentially dangerous or emotionally hurtful, the teacher needs to seem not to be watching in order to encourage the children to work things out on their own, without expecting the teacher to intervene. On the other hand, the teacher wants the children to know that she is aware of what they are doing, because this awareness helps prevent the situation from spinning out of control and gives the children confidence to take risks, knowing that their teacher will jump in if things fall apart. It is only in those moments when the teacher feels that children are on the edge of real danger that she makes her watching more explicit, as when Samata-sensei cautioned Maki to be careful on the climbing bars but didn't tell her to stop. This is the art of Japanese teaching: the art of watching without being either too little or too much present. As one teacher explained to us:

> There is no one right version of *mimamoru*. It does not just mean watching children from a distance, or just letting them know we are watching and that we're ready to go to them if something happens. I believe that what it really means is that we simply exist in the classroom and create a mood that if something happens, the teacher will protect you. It is more like the air around us.

The *mi* in *mimamoru* literally means watching, but as this educator suggests, it also carries the feeling of a presence so all-encompassing and yet so subtle as to be no more noticeable than the atmosphere that surrounds us. Another teacher told us: "It is important that people experience the warmth of being watched over [*mimamorareteiru*]. This is Japanese traditional childcare. From this big loving feeling of knowing one is being watched over and trusted, children figure out their independence."

EMBODYING ATTENTION AND INATTENTION

Marcel Mauss (1934/1973) wrote: "The body is man's first and most natural instrument" (75). Following Mauss, we suggest that *mimamoru* and other Japanese teaching strategies require the deployment of a unique set of bodily techniques. When Japanese teachers do *mimamoru*, they use their body as their principal instrument. *Mimamoru* is not just or primarily a cultural belief of Japanese preschool teachers but also an embodied performance of attention and inattention in space.

A teacher can modulate the degree to which she is present to children by adjusting her location in the classroom and the attitude of her body, with a posture that communicates attention, concern, casualness, or distraction. A skilled teacher strategically performs various levels of paying attention. If children seem too aware of her and dependent on her, the teacher adjusts her gaze and posture to appear to be too busy with a task to pay careful attention to them. In contrast, when a teacher senses children are about to spin out of control, she adjusts her appearance to seem to be paying more attention, such as when Morita calls out, "Kora, kora" (Hey!) in the middle of the teddy bear fight. Teachers also use posture, head tilting, touching, and other body adjustments, in addition to eye contact, to signal levels of attention/inattention.

In the video of the teddy bear fight at Komatsudani, we catch glimpses of

Figure 1.3. Morita walks past the arguing girls.

Figure 1.4a and b. Morita uses her gaze.   Figure 1.5. Kaizuka's eye movements.

Morita in the background adjusting her location in the room, her posture, and her gaze vis-à-vis the fighting girls. We see Morita walking past the girls who are fighting, but not slowing down to intervene (figure 1.3).

Teachers use their gaze (*mokushi*) both to check to see if children are okay and to perform levels of attention and inattention. In a shot that was not included in the twenty-minute video, we see Morita staring from across the room at the group of girls standing near the doorway still fighting over the teddy bear (figure 1.4a and b). She explained to us that this stare was meant to communicate to the girls not that she was concerned about their fighting but that they were not to leave the classroom. In the Madoka video, we see Kaizuka use similar eye movements to indicate to her disobeying students that she is watching them (figure 1.5).

THE TUG OF WAR FIGHT AT MEISEI SCHOOL FOR THE DEAF

Tug of war (*tsunahiki*) is a common playground activity in Japanese preschools and elementary schools. In the video our team shot at Meisei there is a scene on the playground during recess where a cluster of five children holds one end of a rope, the assistant teacher, Kurihara, stands alone on the other side, holding the other end, and the head teacher, Ikeda, stands in the middle, ready to announce the beginning of the contest. A four-year-old girl, Mika, approaches Kurihara-sensei, takes the end of the rope from her, throws it on the ground, and stomps away, as she signs: "It's not fair. My team will lose. The other team has more players." Satoshi, a five-year-old boy holding onto the other end of the rope, comes over to Mika and vigorously disagrees with her assessment, arguing: "But your team has Kurihara-sensei. She is big and strong. And my team has many girls, who are weak." As this argument continues for five minutes or so, another four-year-old girl, Chika, approaches to say something to Mika. Satoshi pushes her away and angrily tells her not to interrupt. Chika, with tears in her eyes, walks away and then signs, "I'm sad" (figures 1.6–1.11).

While Mika and Satoshi are arguing about the sides for the tug of war, the two teachers, Ikeda and Kurihara, sit and stand near them but do not intervene (figure 1.12). Ikeda eventually turns her face away, as if to communicate that she is not available to mediate the dispute.

Toward the end of Mika and Satoshi's heated discussion, Ikeda sits on a bench, ten meters away from the argument. Chika eventually comes over and stands near her. Ikeda explains to Chika that Satoshi has a tendency to

Figure 1.6. Beginning of the tug of war.

Figure 1.7. Mika and Satoshi argue.

Figure 1.8. Chika approaches Mika.

Figure 1.9. Satoshi tells Chika not to interrupt.

Figure 1.10. Satoshi pushes Chika away.

Figure 1.11. Chika says she is sad.

dominate conversations. During her conversation with Chika, Ikeda periodically turns to watch the ongoing discussion between Mika and Satoshi (figure 1.14a and b).

Finally, the tug of war begins, and as Satoshi predicted, Kurihara's team wins. Mika and Satoshi then debrief what has transpired, with Satoshi asking Mika, "Now how do you feel?" and Mika responding, "I see now that you are right that the red team sometimes wins and I shouldn't quit." The children

Figure 1.12. The teachers and children watch Mika and Satoshi's argument.

Figure 1.13. Ikeda turns away from the arguing children.

Figure 1.14a and b. Ikeda and Chika watch the dispute and talk about it.

then apologize to each other and Satoshi says to Mika, "I did a bad thing to Chika and I need to go talk to her." But instead of apologizing, he tells Chika that she should not have interrupted. Chika responds by explaining that she only wanted to say "one little thing" and that he hurt her feelings. Ikeda, sitting just a few feet away, waits and watches, nodding in approval as Chika makes her points.

In a follow-up interview, when we showed Ikeda the tug-of-war scene and asked why she had not intervened in Mika and Satoshi's argument, she replied, in Japanese Sign Language with a series of signs, as shown in figure 1.15a–c. Our JSL interpreter translated these signs into Japanese as the single word *mimamoru*. When we asked as a follow-up question: "You call this approach *mimamoru*?" Ikeda responded: "I don't know how to say it other than maybe [repeating the same series of signs]," which can be literally translated as: "It's yours. I am on the other side of the wall."

Whether we translate Ikeda's signs here as *mimamoru* or as "Handle it yourself. I am staying over here," we can see a clear continuity of pedagogi-

Figure 1.15a–c. "You handle it." "I am . . ." ". . . staying out of it."

cal beliefs and practices between her and her counterparts in hearing preschools. Ikeda's JSL explanation gives us added insight into the logic and
functioning of Japanese preschool teachers' strategy of nonintervention.
In Ikeda's signed explanation, there is no allusion to seeing or guarding,
as there is in the spoken and written versions of *mimamoru*. Ikeda instead
emphasizes a spatial relationship, a dramatic walling off and distancing between her and the fighting children, a location she chooses to occupy, behind
a metaphoric barrier, which precludes her stepping in to intervene and com-
pels the children to deal with the situation themselves. We could argue that
a sense of spatial remove also is present, subtly, in the written and spoken
term, as *mamoru* (to guard) implies watching and protecting from a distance.
This spatial remove is much more explicit in the JSL version. Throughout
this interaction at Meisei, Ikeda, like Morita during the teddy bear fight at
Komatsudani, adjusts her distance from the fighting children, making herself alternatively more and less present.

BUSYNESS

In each of the videos from the Preschool in Three Cultures studies as well as
in the Deaf Kindergarten study we see scenes of Japanese preschool teachers appearing to be too busy with a task to pay careful attention to children's
fights. In the original Preschool in Three Cultures video there is a scene during free-play time after lunch where Hiroki intentionally steps on the hand
of his classmate, Satoshi, making him cry. Fukui is sweeping up when Midori
comes to tell her what Hiroki has done to Satoshi, and Fukui tells her, "If you
are concerned, you do something about it" (figure 1.16). Midori then leads
Satoshi away from Hiroki and advises him to avoid playing with Hiroki in
the future.

Figure 1.16. Fukui sweeps as Midori comes to tattle.

Figure 1.17. Kaizuka interrupts her mediation of a dispute to help a child button a shirt.

By not stopping her sweeping, Fukui lets Midori know that she is too busy to intervene in the dispute, which has the effect of sending Midori back to deal with the situation. When asked later why she had not intervened, Fukui explained that by holding back she provided not only the two fighting boys but Midori and other children in the class as well opportunities to experience emotions and deal with interpersonal conflicts.

Similarly, when the teddy bear fight breaks out in her classroom, Morita's being busy hanging up wet suits and towels suggests to the children that she is unavailable. In the Meisei video we see Ikeda turn her gaze away from two girls arguing near her over some scarfs and busy herself cleaning up dramatic play materials. And during the tug-of-war argument Ikeda periodically turns away from the disputing children to give attention to other children (figure 1.18a). In the Madoka video, in a scene we analyze in detail in chapter 3, we see Kaizuka momentarily turn her attention away from mediating a dispute between two boys to help other children change into the uniforms they wear home (figure 1.17). We suggest that rather than seeing Kaizuka's need to attend to this practical demand as a problematic distraction from dealing with the dispute, her alternating attention between the two tasks works to give the boys opportunities to engage each other both with and without her mediation.

We could say that in these scenes teachers find it difficult to intervene in children's disputes because they are too busy doing routine tasks required of Japanese preschool teachers. At both Madoka and Komatsudani a single teacher has to deal with a class of twenty or more students, without the help of an aide to clean tables, put away swimsuits, and button clothes. During the teddy bear fight, Morita is busy helping children change out of swimsuits, clean up the classroom, and get ready for lunch. During the hair-pulling argument at Madoka, Kaizuka must orchestrate the children's changing into their school uniform and packing up their bags to go home. Because of the demands of the routines and the staffing patterns of the Japanese preschool, these teachers are not just pretending to be busy during these disputes—they are busy. But we suggest that these teachers strategically use their preoccupation with other tasks, along with their positioning in the classroom, posture, and gaze, to artfully alternate their performance of attention and inattention.

LOCATION

Teachers also make themselves more and less available to mediate disputes by strategically adjusting their location. For example, during the tug-of-war argument, Ikeda stood several meters away from the arguing children, close enough to make a suggestion if needed (as she did when she encouraged Mika and Satoshi to talk about it), but far enough away to suggest that she had confidence they could handle the situation on their own (figure 1.12). During an argument between two girls over scarves, Ikeda sat several yards away, alternating between watching the girls argue and being busy folding scarves, and then finally walking away, leaving them to work it out on their own (figure 1.18a–c). Kaizuka used a similar approach when she mediated a fight and said to the boys who had fought, "Think about it," and then dramatically walked away.

The architecture of the buildings and grounds at many Japanese preschools supports the pedagogy of *mimamoru*. For example, Director Machiyama of Madoka explained how he had worked with an architect to design the grounds and buildings so as to provide children with *ajito* (hideaways):

> *Ajito* is a space that children think is their own space. They think that teachers cannot see them when they are in an *ajito* area. But of course, it would be a huge problem if we had a space in the preschool where children were not visible to teachers. The key is that children *think* that it's their own private space.

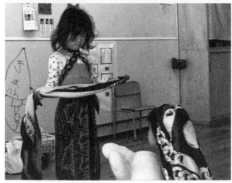

Figure 1.18a–c. Ikeda watches the girls arguing, busies
herself with scarves, and then leaves the girls to work
it out on their own.

Figure 1.19. Boys in an *ajito* location at Madoka.

Director Machiyama suggests that teachers watch children when they enter *ajito* places (figure 1.19), without drawing the children's attention to the fact that they are being watched.

TOUCH

Japanese preschool teachers often use touch to intervene wordlessly and unobtrusively when children are misbehaving or are feeling stressed (Burke and Duncan 2015, 66–67). There are examples in our videos. In the hair-pulling incident, when both of the boys insisted the other had started the fight and then grew silent, Kaizuka touched them rather than using more words. She reached her right arm around one boy and held his waist while looking in his eyes, patted the other boy's head, tapped a boy on the chest, and gripped a boy's arm (figures 1.20a and b, 1.21a and b, and 1.22a and b). Later in the day of the teddy bear fight, when Nao again snatched the bear from another girl and refused to give it back, Morita watched for a while and then came closer and cued Nao to release her grip by touching her hand (figure 1.23). Ikeda did not intervene during Chika and Satoshi's argument, but she squatted close to the children, alongside Chika, who drew needed moral support by stroking her teacher's hair (figure 1.24a–c).

Figure 1.20a and b. Holding.

Figure 1.21a and b. Patting.

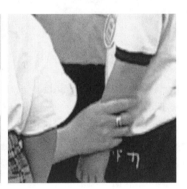

Figure 1.22a and b. Gripping.

POSTURE

During her mediation of the hair-pulling fight Kaizuka provokes the boys to do some soul searching by using a variety of techniques of the body including using her hands to position the boys close to her and to each other; adjusting her location and gaze vis-à-vis the boys, at times moving away, at

Figure 1.23. Morita touches Nao's hand.

Figure 1.24a–c. Chika gets support from stroking Ikeda's hair.

times looking away; touching them to get their attention, emphasize a point, and to draw them close to her; expressing emotion and concern with her facial expressions; and staring into the boys' eyes, which she was able to do by kneeling so that her eyes were lower than theirs (figure 1.25a and b). This is just one of the many examples in our videos where teachers squat, kneel, or sit on a low bench in postures that suggest that they are relaxed and in no hurry. By squatting, Kaizuka engages with the boys from a posture not of authority but of sincere concern.

In figure 1.12 we see Kurihara-sensei squatting among the tug-of-war participants, a posture that suggests she is willingly to wait for as long as it is going to take for Mika and Satoshi to settle their disagreement. Squatting is a very informal register of sitting, so much so that one term for it is *yakuza suwari* (sitting like a gangster). When Kurihara viewed the video she commented that her squatting was *gyōgi ga warui* (bad manners). We interpret

Figure 1.25a and b: Kaizuka kneels to mediate the boys' argument.

Figure 1.26. Ikeda squats.

this comment to mean not that she thinks it is wrong to be so informal with children, but that it is embarrassing to be seen in such an informal posture in front of visitors or in a video.

In the middle of the tug-of-war argument Ikeda shifts from watching while standing (figure 1.12), to squatting (figure 1.26), to sitting on a low step (figure 1.14a and b). Her squatting, like Kurihara's, indicates to the children that she is not about to intervene and that she is prepared for the interaction to continue for a while.

TIME

Each of the bodily techniques of performing *mimamoru* we have discussed above requires the artful use of timing. It is duration that distinguishes a glance from a look from a stare. Duration also distinguishes a tap from a pat from a firm grip of a shoulder. Squatting also carries a temporal dimension, as it communicates settling in to let time pass, as opposed to postures that suggest a readiness to act.

Another notion of time at work in the practice of *mimamoru* is the time children need to develop, and the patience teachers should have in interactions with children. For example, when we asked Morita about Nao's crying in the fighting scene, she explained:

> Her birthday is in February [the Japanese school year starts in April and ends in March]. She started here only last February. Other children came here when they were one or two years old. So it can be said that she was a new child at that moment [when the research team videotaped her classroom]. But she has changed a lot since she came here, and she will be different if you return later this year. That's why I let them fight.

Morita thinks about the value of her nonintervention from a long-term perspective, in Japanese, *nagai me* (long eyes). During the time Nao has been at Komatsudani, Morita has seen Nao's progress in social skills, and she knows that Nao has another eighteen months in her classroom to continue her development (at Komatsudani as at many other Japanese preschools, teachers stay with the same group of children for three years). Fukui-sensei in the original Preschool in Three Cultures study said she could be patient with Hiroki, who was constantly misbehaving, because she would have him as her student for another two years and he was gradually improving. Preschool teachers can watch and wait because they have this long perspective. A *hoikuen* teacher in a focus group said after watching the Madoka Yōchien video: "This is difficult! How can we know children well enough to watch them?" For her, it was difficult to watch the children in the video in a meaningful way (to *mimamoru*) because she did not have enough time to know these children and therefore to take a long perspective. Or perhaps she was also implying that it is more difficult for *yōchien* teachers, who have children in their class for only two years, to know their students as well as can *hoikuen* teachers, who are often in charge of children from infancy onward.

In chapter 5 we argue that just as teachers take the long perspective and give children time and space to develop their capacities to mediate social interactions, so do preschools give new teachers time and space to develop their professional expertise. As Director Kumagai told us, "It takes at least five years for a teacher to learn to do *mimamoru*."

THE RECIPROCITY OF *MIMAMORU*

Mimamoru means not only to hold back from intervening but also to "keep an eye on" someone needing guidance. Rather than being an intrusive or surveilling gaze, *mimamoru* is connected to a nurturing concern, and to *amae*, to the knowledge that we all need help from others. A younger employee will often say to his supervisor or a student to her mentor, "Mimamotte kudasai" (Please keep watching over me). The more competent member of a dyad will say to someone younger or less competent: "Mimamotteru" (I'll keep a watchful eye on you). What matters most here is not age and status, but rather that the person who does the *mimamoru* is at least potentially able to help the other person with something he or she can't do alone. *Mimamoru* can be reciprocal. It is therefore common not only for students to seek the watchful concern of their teacher, but also for teachers, even at the preschool level, to ask their students to keep an eye on them to prevent them from making absentminded errors. For example, during morning opening, if children catch their teacher making a mistake about the day or date, the teacher will respond, "Mitete" (Please keep an eye on me), implying that she depends on the class to help her with their attention. We witnessed a similar example at Senzan Yōchien, where a group of children told Director Kumagai that their teacher had neglected to close the door of the class birdcage. Director Kumagai replied, "Mitette, ne" (Watch her, okay?), meaning that is their responsibility, rather than hers, to help their teacher avoid such mistakes.

These examples emphasize the sociality implicit in *mimamoru*, a practice that we suggest knits society together by emphasizing mutual responsibility for watching and caring for each other, a topic we return to in chapter 3, in our discussion of *seken no me* (the eyes of society). *Mimamoru* is also connected with *amae*, acting in a way that produces in others a desire to offer nurturance or help. To speak or act in a way that suggests a desire for someone to watch over you is to ask people to help, but not in a direct way. Teachers need to keep their eye on children and children on teachers because, as Bakhtin suggests in *Art and Answerability* (1990), we cannot truly see ourselves objectively or evaluate the effects of our actions. We cannot see ourselves against the backdrop of the larger context of our lives. In this sense, *mimamoru*—watching others and being watched—is a core component of sociality, a component that is emphasized in the pedagogy of the Japanese preschool.

Chapter 2

—

The Pedagogy of Feelings

Figure 2.1.

SAD FISH AND LONELY CARROTS

At a preschool in Kyoto a teacher stands in front of her class of four-year-olds and holds up brightly colored sheets of origami paper:

> We're going to make fish today. First we make a triangle. And then fold in both sides, just like when you make a tulip. Then fold the two corners in, like this. And one more fold, like this. Got it? Good! Now it looks like a fish. But it looks so sad and lonely [*sabishii*] without a mouth or eyes. What should we do? I'll take a marker and draw an eye on my fish, like this.

At lunchtime at Komatsudani a teacher notices that many of the children have finished their meat and rice and dessert, but left their carrots untouched. Speaking to a boy in a theatrical voice loud enough for the whole class to hear, the teacher says, "Poor Mr. Carrot! You ate Mr. Hamburger, Mr. Rice, and Mr. Orange, but you haven't eaten any of Mr. Carrot. Don't you think he feels lonely [*sabishii*]?"

On one level, the teachers' actions here are easy to understand and seem to require no ethnographic explanation. In the first example the teacher encourages her students to add facial features to their paper fish; in the second, the teacher urges students to eat their vegetables. What needs explaining is why these teachers evoke such heavy emotion to achieve such banal goals. Why, for example, bring up loneliness to get a child to eat her vegetables or to get children to put eyes on their paper fish? In this chapter we analyze the Mr. Carrot and the paper fish incidents alongside other activities involving emotion we have observed in Japanese preschools and use these analyses to construct a theory of the pedagogy of feelings and empathy in Japanese early childhood education.

THE CULTURAL SALIENCE OF LONELINESS

The word used by the teachers in the fish and carrot examples is *sabishii*, which carries a meaning close to the English word "lonely," but with a stronger sense of being forlorn or desolate. In the contexts above, perhaps the best translation would be "feeling left out and therefore sad." The carrot is sad because he has been passed over and left alone on the plate and not been allowed to join his lunch compatriots, the hamburger, rice, and orange, in being eaten.

To most U.S. early childhood educators who have watched the Komatsudani video, describing foods as lonely seems like an odd way to encourage a child to eat his vegetables. This is one of those situations where insider informants are unable to offer a profound explanation because the practice in question is so ordinary and the logic behind it tacit. Japanese early childhood educators we asked about the lunch scene said that this approach to get children to eat is commonly used in preschools and in homes, but that it carries no special or deep meaning. We suggest that being a member of the group is so highly valued in Japanese culture in general and in preschool pedagogy in particular that missing out on the opportunity of being eaten alongside one's comrades makes one an object of pity and concern, even if you are a carrot and your comrades other inanimate objects. The implicit logic here is that children will accept the fanciful premise that items of food have feelings, they will empathize with the neglected, sad carrot, and eat him in an act of sympathy that will allow him to rejoin his old lunchbox companions. Getting young children to comply by appealing for consideration of the feelings of vegetables as well as people has been described in the literature as a strategy used by Japanese parents (Conroy et al. 1980; Hess et al. 1986). A Japanese researcher told us that she encourages her one-year-old to nurse by saying, "You've eaten from Mrs. Left Breast. How about Mrs. Right Breast. Don't you think she's feeling sad?"

The paper fish that lacks facial features is lonely in a somewhat different sense; it is not abandoned but incomplete, and therefore sad. Again, Morita and other Japanese early childhood educators we interviewed about the videotape saw no special significance in her comment about the fish's being lonely because it lacked eyes. Our interpretation is that the use of *sabishii* here to describe the fish should be understood as reflecting Japanese aesthetic as well as psychological constructs. The root of *sabishii* is *sabi*, which means "alone" and which is used in Japanese aesthetic discourse, usually coupled with the word *wabi*, to refer to an intense, highly valued mood of austerity, simplicity, longing, and sadness evoked in or by a work of art. The term *wabi* originally referred to "the misery of living alone in nature" (Koren 1994). As with the English word "hermit," this loneliness is not viewed as entirely negative and is associated with a morally admirable aestheticism found in Zen, which embraces simplicity and rejects materialism. As Andrew Juniper (2003) writes, "If an object or expression can bring about, within us, a sense of serene melancholy and a spiritual longing, then that object could be said to be *wabi sabi* (11)." Jamie Hubbard (2008) writes, "Both of these expressions [*wabi* and *sabi*] can be understood to refer to a sense of the smallness or finite-ness of the individual in the face of the infinite." Like *wabi-sabi*, *sabishii* should be understood as a sad emotion, but one that is highly valued, cultivated, and savored. Morita's use of the word *sabishii* describes the feeling state not only of the eyeless fish but also of the person who gazes sympathetically on this work of (unfinished) art. This doubling of feeling, this identification of an observed object with the self, is the root of the meaning of empathy, which was an aesthetic term before it became a psychological one (Titchener 1909). Morita points out to the children that the fish without eyes produces a sense of loneliness in those who view it, loneliness that can be reduced by adding an eye and making the fish more complete.

AMAE

In the beginning of the video of "A Day at Komatsudani" we see Nao, the youngest and most recently enrolled child in Morita's class, arrive at school with her mother and three-month-old brother. At the school gate, when her

Figure 2.2. Nao clings to her mom.

Figure 2.3. Maki holds Nao's hand.

Figure 2.4. Nao cries as Maki looks on.

mother says goodbye and attempts to leave, Nao protests and clings to her arm. Morita and Nao's classmate, Maki, approach and encourage Nao to let go of her mother's arm (figure 2.2). Eventually, the two girls hold hands and walk together to the playground where they join other girls to play (figure 2.3). A bit later, inside the classroom, Nao gets into the teddy bear fight with Seiko, Reiko, and Yoko discussed in the previous chapter (figure 2.4). When we asked Morita why she did not intervene in this fight, she emphasized that she viewed the fight as a positive expression of the desire in both Nao and the other girls for social interaction and a valuable opportunity for everyone involved to experience and work through emotions.

We suggest that Nao's clinging to her mother when she's dropped off at school, fighting with the other girls for possession of the teddy bear, and then whining when she loses the fight can be read as what Takeo Doi would categorize as immature expressions of *amae*. In his 1973 book *The Anatomy of Dependence*, Doi argued that *amae* is a key concept for understanding the

Japanese psyche because it reflects the high value placed in Japan on expressions of vulnerability. *Amae* is often translated into English as "dependence," but this translation makes *amae* come across as too passive. To emphasize the agency in *amae* we prefer as a translation "acting in a way that invites help and concern from others" (Hayashi, Karasawa, and Tobin 2009).

Nao wants to be a member of the group of girls, but has a limited repertoire of ways to engage them. She appeals for inclusion by displaying *amae* in an immature form that the older girls understand and respond to. Standing at the gate each morning clinging to her mother and crying can be read as a show of forlornness and *amae* intended not just for her mother (who Nao knows will soon leave despite her protestations) but also or primarily for her teacher and especially for her classmates, whose attention and acceptance she craves. Nao's determination to have control of the teddy bear can be read similarly as a display of *amae* that communicates to the other girls Nao's immaturity, loneliness, and desire for connection.

Nao's whiny, aggressive expressions of *amae* and the other girls' sometimes gentle and sometimes harsh responses are immature, or, to use the preferred term of Japanese early childhood educators, *kodomo-rashii*, which literally means "childlike." It could be said that such childlike expressions of *amae* are *amae* in its purest form. The quintessential expression of *amae* is a not quite yet talking or walking infant reaching her arms in the air as a request to be picked up. Drawing on psychoanalytic theories of the development of the self and object relations, Doi suggests that infants under six months old are not usually described as doing *amae* because they do not yet have a sense of themselves as separate and therefore do not yet experience the existential loneliness and the conscious desire for the other that are the core motivation that drives *amae* and that makes it a key force in binding society together. The primary developmental lesson to be learned in the first few years of life in Japan is not independence but how to overcome one's essential, existential separation and loneliness through interdependency (Caudill and Plath 1966). Expressions of loneliness and sadness are key components of *amae*, and *amae*, the ability to make people want to care for you, is a key component of interdependency and therefore a fundamental building block of Japanese sociality.

The development of sociality is a central goal of the Japanese preschool curriculum, which emphasizes the cultivation in young children of group mindedness (*shūdan shugi*) and a social orientation (*shakai seikatsu*). Loneliness expresses a desire for connection to others, and leads to seeking companionship and membership in a group. It is Nao's loneliness that leads to her expressions of *amae* that in turn work to bring her into connection with the group of girls. It is for these reasons that Morita views Nao's loneliness and sadness as positive emotions and her expressions of *amae*, no matter how immaturely expressed, as prosocial.

OMOIYARI

In our interviews, teachers often paired the term *amae* with the term *omoi-yari* (empathy). This pairing suggests that displays of loneliness, sadness, helplessness, and other emotionally vulnerable states are reciprocally tied to *omoiyari* (empathy) to form a circuit of emotional exchange, which, although not unique to Japan or to the Japanese preschool, have a particular cultural patterning and salience in Japan and in the Japanese approach to the socialization of emotions. This is consistent with Catherine Lutz's (1988) suggestion that emotions need to be understood not only or primarily as intrapsychic phenomena experienced by individuals but as phenomena that are interpersonal and social. Lutz explains how expressions of anger in Ifaluk society, in Micronesia, produce responses of anxiety in others and expressions of happiness produce responses of jealousy:

> Ifaluk cultural logic elucidates how each emotion presupposes the other in the above pairs. These exchanges, which are more or less culturally stereotyped, are socially achieved scenarios, and they are culturally interpreted and learned. This view of emotions more adequately reflects the emotional flow of everyday social interaction. (212)

The same is the case, we argue, in Japanese preschools for expressions of dependency and emotional vulnerability (*amae*) and responses of empathy (*omoiyari*). *Amae* can function in an interpersonal interaction only when its reciprocal, *omoiyari*—the ability and willingness to respond to the needs of others—is also present.

Takie Lebra (1976) defines *omoiyari* as "the ability and willingness to feel what others are feeling, to vicariously experience the pleasure and pain that they are undergoing, and to help them satisfy their wishes" (38). Lebra, who views *omoiyari* as a key component of what she calls "social preoccupation" and "interactional relativism," emphasizes the cultural value placed in Japan on attending to and even anticipating the needs and feelings of others. In other words, to be a good person in Japan requires putting a lot of time and energy into figuring out what others are feeling and thinking.

Some Japanese-English dictionaries translate *omoiyari* as "consideration." In some contexts, this is a good translation, as "considerate," like *omoiyari*, suggests a combination of thought and action. To be considerate means to be sensitive to the feelings of another and to act accordingly. But we prefer to translate *omoiyari* as "empathy" because this conveys more of the emotional depth of the term and better connects with the literature on the development of sociality in young children.

Omoiyari is commonly described as a major goal of Japanese childrearing and early childhood education (Kojima 1986; Olson, Kashiwagi, and Crystal 2001). In *The Kindergarten Education Guidelines*, the first item listed is "Omoiyari no kokoro o taisetsu ni shimashō" (Let's think about the importance of *omoiyari*). A survey used in the original *Preschool in Three Cultures* study (Tobin, Wu, and Davidson 1989) showed that Japanese early childhood educators rated the item "sympathy/empathy/concern for others" as the most important thing for children to learn in preschool.

In the Japanese anthropological and psychological literature there are discussions of the cultural centrality of the concepts of *amae* and *omoiyari*, but little discussion of the connection between the two or how both are linked to feelings and expressions of *sabishii*. We suggest that *amae* and *omoiyari* should be viewed as reciprocally related. There can be no *amae* without the expectation of *omoiyari* and no *omoiyari* without a perceived need for *amae*, any more than an economy could have buying without selling. If one does *amaeru* (acts in a way intended to solicit help or attention from another), and the other is not able or willing to respond to this appeal, then the *amae* loses its meaning, like the sound of the proverbial tree falling in the forest. Of course in preschools and elsewhere sometimes there are expressions of longing and dependence that fail to find an empathetic response, and there are empathetic gestures offered that are unwanted and even resented (there is a word for this in Japanese—*osekkai*, which means to offer unwanted assistance). But the failures or breakdowns in the circuit that connects *amae* to *omoiyari* are the exceptions that prove the rule of their reciprocal connection.

In the Preschool in Three Cultures videotapes we see a few examples of teachers teaching empathy directly, mostly in the form of introducing and reinforcing a vocabulary of emotions, as in Morita's discussion with the children of the fish that is sad because it lacks eyes. Alongside such direct approaches, Japanese preschool teachers support the development of empathy in young children by providing them with multiple opportunities to experience social complexity and to interact to work out authentic (as opposed to teacher posed) social and emotional dilemmas with a minimum of adult mediation.

Empathy has three major aspects: intuitive emotional understanding of others, sympathy, and prosocial behavior. In other words, prosocial behavior requires the ability to read the emotions of another, to feel concern, and then to do something about it. In the Komatsudani videotape, we see examples of children working on all three of these aspects of empathy. The responses of Maki and the other girls to Nao's expressions of loneliness can be understood as expressions of *omoiyari*. Maki helping Nao to separate from her mother at the school gate by taking her hand and encouraging her to come play clearly qualifies as empathy: Maki accurately identifies or reads Nao's loneliness and expression of *amae*, feels sorry for her, and then intervenes in an effective way. We suggest that the older girls' responses to Nao's refusal to share the teddy bear also qualify as acts of empathy, even if the form of these responses is harsh and seemingly unsympathetic. Letting Nao have the bear rather than taking it away from her might seem on the surface like a more empathetic response. But Morita explained that Nao's real desire is not for the bear; it is for inclusion in the social life of the other girls. As soon as it ceases to be an object of struggle, Nao and her classmates lose interest in the bear, which is, after all, just a stuffed animal. If the older girls were to allow Nao to have the teddy bear, this would be an act of sympathy, but not empathy, as it would be a misreading of Nao's real desire, which is for social interaction. Instead of letting her have the bear, the older girls take it from her when they judge that it is not her turn to have it and then use this occasion to chastise and correct her. These actions may look harsh to adults, but they are appropriate and effective responses to Nao's desire to be included in the social life of the older girls. If what is being felt is loneliness and what is needed is attention, then the children's responses are appropriate and effective.

A PEDAGOGY OF RESTRAINT

Morita supports the girls' interactions by artfully not intervening and, when she does intervene, doing so strategically and with restraint. As we discuss in chapter 3, Japanese teachers view not intervening not as the absence of acting, but as a pedagogical action that requires restraint and judgment. We can say that Morita's nonintervention is itself an act of empathy—to break up the fight would be to misread Nao's desire and the girls' response and to give Nao and the other girls something they don't want (adult interference).

We can also suggest that Morita's hesitancy to intervene in the children's disputes reflects a cultural pedagogical belief that lessons in emotional development and social skills are better learned from the experience of interacting with peers than from didactic instruction or from adult-child dyadic interactions. The large class size and high student/teacher ratios of the Japanese preschool classroom do not allow the teacher to give frequent one-on-one attention to individual students. Indeed, Tobin, Wu, and Davidson (1987) have argued that this is part of the cultural rationale for keeping the student/teacher ratios high in Japanese preschools. If the ratios were lower and class size smaller, teachers would be more tempted to intervene and as a result students would miss out on opportunities to interact with peers in emotion-filled scenarios without adult mediation.

EMBODIED EXPERIENCES OF EMOTION

Underlying the low-intervention approach Japanese teachers use to support children's social-emotional development is a belief in the value of learning about emotions through embodied experience. In her book *Inside Japanese Classrooms*, Nancy Sato (2004) emphasizes the value Japanese teachers give to experiential learning, and she parses three Japanese words that all can be translated into English as "experience":

> One is *kemmon* or *kembun*; the word is a combination of the two *kanji*, "to see" and "to hear." This is experience through the eyes and ears. . . . Another word is *keiken*, which is experience through the passing of time. . . . The third word is used in contrast to *keiken* and signifies experience through the total body: *taiken*. The two *kanji* for *taiken* are the words for "body" and "testing," so investigation through actual experience involving the whole body and all its senses is a more inclusive way to experience. Several principals and teachers remarked that the more important for true learning is *taiken*. The significance of the total body in learning is recognized in Japanese educational thought and underlies much of the educational practice I observed. (87)

Sato's findings on the centrality of learning through experience in Japanese elementary education are consistent with our findings on the way

Japanese preschool teachers talk about how young children develop social-emotional competence through experience. For example, when we asked Morita what children learn from fighting, she answered: "Children come to know a range of feelings. One day, children might experience *itte kanashii* [saying something that hurts someone's feelings and, as a result, makes the speaker sad], and another day children might experience *iwarete kanashii* [somebody says something to them that makes them sad]. Children cannot understand these feelings without having direct experiences [*taiken*]." Morita's colleague, Nogami, commented on the teddy bear fight scene: "This is the way that children get to know their strength, how much force to use when they hit people. They learn that if they use too much power, it hurts people. They need to experience this with their body; otherwise, they'll never know their strength." The word both of these teachers used for experience, *taiken*, emphasizes the embodied nature of these emotional experiences.

Catherine Lewis (1984, 78) presents the example of a physical fight between two five-year-old boys that the teacher responds to, not by breaking it up, but instead by encouraging the boy who was losing to cry, rather than to attempt to suppress his tears and thereby obscure his feelings. The teacher's logic here is that social interactions among classmates require a clear communication of feeling, and that if one child in an altercation cries or in other ways communicates pain, frustration, or emotional vulnerability, this will work to elicit an empathetic response from one or more others (Lewis 1995, 126–30). In situations where one child is hurting another, if a teacher feels the need to intervene, her intervention will often take the form, not, as in U.S. preschools, of telling the aggressor to stop or encouraging him to be more empathetic, but instead of encouraging the victim to present his distress more clearly, so as to elicit the desired empathetic response. The mastery of such complex forms of interpersonal interaction is believed to develop less as a result of teacher interventions than through the accrual of embodied experiences.

We see another variation on this pedagogical approach in a scene in the Madoka video where Kaizuka mediates a fight between two boys. In the video, as the children are preparing to go home, we see Nobu, in tears, approach Kaizuka (figures 2.5–10):

NOBU: Yusuke pulled my hair.
KAIZUKA: Why did you do that, Yusuke?

Figure 2.5. "Yusuke pulled my hair."

Figure 2.6. "Is that true?"

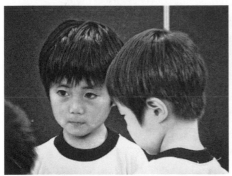

Figure 2.7. "Think about it."

Figure 2.8. "God, too, is watching."

Figure 2.9. "Do you have something to say?"

Figure 2.10. "I'm sorry."

YUSUKE: Cuz Nobu-kun pinched me.

KAIZUKA: You say he pinched you first? Is that true?

YUSUKE: No.

KAIZUKA: That's strange.

NOBU: He walked by and pulled my hair.

KAIZUKA: And then you pinched him? Nobu, did you pinch him or not? You pinched him, right? I don't like this. God, too, is watching. Do you understand? Think about it. And when you are ready to tell the truth, come talk to me. Think about it. I am more bothered by your lying than by what you did. Think about it [as Kaizuka turns her attention momentarily to a girl asking for help with a button, Yusuke wanders away]. Yusuke, come back, we're not done.

YUSUKE [with tears in his eyes, whimpering]: I did it first.

KAIZUKA: It's really important to say you're sorry when you do bad things. I've done bad things to friends, but then I realized I was wrong and apologized. If you apologize, you feel much better. Do you understand? Do you have something to say?

YUSUKE: I'm sorry.

NOBU: That's okay.

KAIZUKA [to NOBU]: You, also, have to say, "sorry."

NOBU: I'm sorry.

YUSUKE: That's okay.

KAIZUKA: You'll have to change your clothes quickly. Everyone is waiting for you.

Kaizuka's anguished tone of voice, facial expressions, and bodily comportment reflect not her actual emotional state during the interaction, but instead a performance of emotion intended not only to get the boys to tell the truth and then to apologize but also and perhaps even more important to get them to express and acknowledge the sadness that comes from fighting with a friend. We are suggesting not that she is being deceptive or dishonest with the boys and feigning concern she does not feel, but rather that she is performing an exaggerated, embodied version of this concern to provoke in the boys a desired physical and emotional response. One clue is how, when she is interrupted periodically by children needing help with buttons, she either calmly tells them she is busy or nonchalantly does their buttons while continuing to mediate the fighting boys' interaction (figure 2.11a). This suggests that her intensity and emotionality with the two four-year-old boys was a carefully crafted technique, a performance that, eventually, had the intended effect. She told us: "I was concerned by their lying, but no, I was not upset. It's a typical kind of interaction among children this age, isn't it?"

There are many examples in our videos of Kaizuka and other teachers

Figure 2.11. Kaizuka buttons a shirt while mediating the dispute.

Figure 2.12. Kaizuka performs sadness by lowering her eyes and using her hands to mime crying.

using their faces, voices, and bodies to perform exaggerated versions of emotions. One, discussed at the beginning of this chapter, is Morita expressing with her voice and face the sadness of an origami fish with no eyes. In the Madoka video there is a scene of Kaizuka saying to the children: "I won't see you during summer vacation, which will make me very sad. So I'll write to you." As she says this she does a theatrical, embodied performance of her anticipated sadness by lowering her eyes and then using her hands to mime crying (figure 2.12).

At Meisei School for the Deaf, in a scene where Ikeda reads the children a story about a donkey who stays up all night making backpacks for his friends, at one juncture of the story she points to a drawing in the book showing the sad donkey tailor and then asks the children: "Why does Mr. Donkey have this face? They made a plan to go on a field trip, but Mr. Donkey totally for-

Figure 2.13a and b. Ikeda performs the donkey's sad face, and children show concern.

got to make his own backpack!" As she says (signs) this, she makes a concerned, sad face that mirrors that of the donkey, a face the children in the class in turn mimic (figure 2.13a and b).

PHYSICAL FEELINGS

Teachers emphasize giving children experiences not only of feelings such as sadness, anger, and frustration, but also of feelings that are more directly sensory, such as hunger, tiredness, and being cold, dirty, and wet. The emphasis is on the experience not only of being muddy, for example, but also of *feeling* muddy; and not just of taking a fieldtrip carrying a heavy (for a preschooler) backpack, but also of feeling the fatigue and muscle ache (as well as the sense of accomplishment) that come from such bodily exertion (figure 2.14).

Preschool in Three Cultures contains a description of a morning at Komatsu-dani Hoikuen when Director Yoshizawa led an impromptu excursion to a muddy field near the school for the morning exercise activity (*taisō*):

TOBIN: Why did you take the children to that place for *taiso*?
YOSHIZAWA: These days children only know how to play if they are given special toys and playground equipment. We took them to that field so they could learn how to play without special equipment. The idea was for them to discover that they can have fun even on an empty lot.

Figure 2.14. Carrying a big load.

TOBIN: Did you know it would be so muddy?

YOSHIZAWA: It's because I knew it was muddy that I chose to take
them there. I went by there this morning and saw the mud and
decided to bring the older children. You noticed that most of them
were afraid of getting dirty? These days, many children don't
know how to be children. Especially *hoikuen* children like ours,
who are in school all day, every day. They grow up not having the
opportunity to play in the mud if we don't arrange for them to get
it here with us.

As Eyal Ben-Ari (1997), Daniel Walsh (2002; 2004), and Rachael Burke
and Judith Duncan (2015) have emphasized, there is a premium in Japanese preschools on embodied experiences including running, jumping, and
climbing; fighting; engaging with the natural world; and gathering so close
together that bodies touch, which Ben-Ari calls "grouping."

In the Komatsudani video there are shots of children playing in the dirt,
getting wet (figure 2.15), and sleeping together (figure 2.16). In the Madoka
video there are shots of a boy filling his shoe with water, boys playing with
beetles, and a silly song about the stinky smell of a sparrow's poop (figure
2.17). We happened to visit Meisei once on the day of the rice planting festival (figure 2.18). The teachers were dressed in shorts and t-shirts, the older
preschool children in their underwear, and the younger ones were naked.
Everyone got muddy from head to toe.

Figure 2.15. Getting wet.

Figure 2.16. Sleeping together.

Figure 2.17. Poop smells stinky.

Figure 2.18. Rice planting.

The value placed on experiencing physical feelings extends even to being physically hurt and hurting someone. As a preschool director in Kyoto told us: "Little injuries protect against a big injury. So it's okay if children get hurt a little bit. To let them have a little injury, but not a big injury, this is our job as a teacher." The emic pedagogical principle here is that children learn through bodily experience, rather than only via words and mind. And this embodied learning is a collective rather than individual experience. Children develop a sense of being members of a society through the sharing of such bodily activities as fighting, crying, getting muddy, and co-sleeping.

LONELINESS, EMPATHY, AND SOCIALITY

A key pedagogical goal of Japanese preschool teachers is to provide young children with opportunities to experience feelings. All feelings are not of equal value. *Sabishii* is emphasized much more than, for example, anger or embarrassment. An example can be found in *The Kindergarten Education Guidelines*, which state that a key curricular goal for children is "sharing enjoyment and sadness [*sabishiisa*] through active involvement in relationships with friends." We suggest that sadness/loneliness is so highly valued because this feeling is seen to provoke responses of *omoiyari* and to fuel the desire for sociality. Loneliness and sociality are reciprocally connected: Feeling lonely motivates people to seek the company of others. Expressions of loneliness, in turn, provoke the empathic response of inviting the lonely person to join the group. Shared experiences of talking about and both directly and vicariously experiencing loneliness provide a sense of intersubjectivity that strengthens group ties.

Children need to learn to express their loneliness and other needs in terms of *amaeru*, which means to act in a way that invites empathetic responses. If you feel lonely but do not show it, or if you need help but hide your helplessness, you preclude the possibility of an empathetic, prosocial response from others. Learning to express *amae* is therefore a crucial developmental task for young children. Children need in preschool to have ample opportunities to experience both *amae* and *omoiyari*, that is, opportunities to express their needs, to have their needs responded to by teachers and peers, and to respond to the needs of others.

Our work here follows, supports, and extends the line of research conducted by psychological anthropologists that argues that emotions need to be understood as relational (Lutz 1988; Bender et al. 2007). The emotions that Japanese preschool pedagogy focuses on—the triad of *sabishii, amae,* and *omoiyari* (loneliness, interdependence, and empathy)—are relational both in the sense of being interpersonal and intersubjective rather than only or primarily as intrapsychic, and in the sense of being not discrete phenomena but instead tied together in sequences of expression and response.

Chapter 3

—

The Pedagogy of
Peripheral Participation

Figure 3.1.

"LOOK. THERE IS A GALLERY"

One of the methods we used for this study was to reanalyze the video-cued interviews from the Preschool in Three Cultures Revisited study. In the course of reanalyzing these transcripts, we noticed something that we had missed before in comments from Director Ritsuko Kumagai of Senzan Yōchien in Kyoto. As Director Kumagai watched the hair-pulling fight scene at Madoka, she commented: "Look, there is a *gyarari* [gallery]. Fights are important for the children who are *not* fighting. Teachers should pay attention to them and consider what *they* are learning."

As we attended afresh to Director Kumagai's words, and especially to her use of the English loan word *gyarari*, we came to the realization that in our previous analyses of this and other scenes of fighting in Japanese preschool classrooms we had missed something important. In our focus on the children directly involved in the fights (the children doing the pushing, hitting, pinching, crying, tattle-telling, and mediating), we had failed to notice the children on the periphery of these scenes, children who watched the fights without (at least from our perspective) being actively involved. These are the children Kumagai referred to as a "gallery." In the course of shooting and editing the videos and using them as interviewing cues we had watched these fight scenes literally hundreds of times without noticing the galleries that formed around the fighters and mediators, and without considering what these peripherally participating children might be experiencing, learning, or contributing (Hayashi and Tobin 2011).

In this chapter we present a reanalysis of the hair-pulling fight and other scenes of fighting in Japanese preschools. This reanalysis requires us to refocus our attention, both metaphorically and literally, from those fighting and mediating in the center of the frame to those in the surrounding gallery of peripherally participating observers. We present a Japanese emic perspective, featuring the words and concepts used by Japanese practitioners to explain their beliefs and practices concerning children who play a peripheral role in fights. We read this Japanese emic perspective alongside and, in some cases, against theories of legitimate peripheral participation, observational learning, social learning, self-regulation, and panopticism.

THE HAIR-PULLING FIGHT RETOLD

We can retell the story of the hair-pulling fight, this time from the point of view of the *gyarari* children:

> As the children are changing from their gym clothes to their school uniforms in preparation for going home, the classroom teacher calls over two boys, to mediate a dispute involving accusations of pushing and hair pulling. Several children, in the midst of changing, look on at the interaction from various locations around the room. Aya, who happens to be standing near the boys and teacher, turns toward them and watches their interaction attentively, looking back and forth from one to the other as she unbuttons her shirt. Masa, wearing only his underpants, uniform shirt in hand, looks on intently from across the room and then approaches, apparently too transfixed to complete the process of changing his clothes. Yamato stands just behind the teacher and looks over her shoulder at the arguing boys. Masa, Hiroto, and Sakura form a semicircle around the teacher and the two boys. Hiroto and Sakura come closer as the teacher speaks to one of the arguing

boys. Sakura, standing right behind the teacher with her hands held firmly at her sides, leans forward to listen. Masa, still in his underwear, and Sakura come closer, with pensive expressions. As the teacher's intervention in the fight continues, other children who have finished changing into their uniforms approach and look and listen. As the interaction nears a resolution, Misaki approaches from the left and Hiroto steps up close and reaches out and places a comforting hand on Nobu's back. Yuki and Hiro lean in as the teacher says to the disputing boys, "God, too, is watching." As she taps Yusuke's head to emphasize her point, Daisuke watching nearby imitates the teacher's gesture.

Over the course of this ten-minute interaction, not a moment has gone by without at least one other child approaching and attending to the event. Aya, Masa, Hiroto, Daisuke, Yamato, Yuki, Sakura, Hiro, and Misaki have taken on a variety of stances, from watching and listening from a distance, to coming in close, to reaching out to touch and pat the fighting boys. The teacher has several times reminded watching children to continue changing their clothes, but she has never shooed them away or told them it is not their business.

THE HAIR-PULLING FIGHT REFOCUSED

A visual reanalysis of the fight scene requires both a conceptual and a literal shifting of focus. The shots of the scene in the video *A Day at Madoka Yōchien* are mostly close-ups and medium shots of the teacher and two boys (figures 3.2–3). But in some of the close-up and medium shots as well as in the few wider shots (figure 3.4), if we shift our attention away from the protagonists, we see other children present, on the periphery of the frame. Although these children are physically present in these shots, before hearing Director Kumagai's comment we somehow did not notice them. What prevents these children in the *gyarari* from being seen? And what can we do to render them visible? What is needed are strategies that support a refocusing of attention, strategies that can draw our eyes to characters we first assume are peripheral to the action (Hayashi and Tobin 2012).

An approach we have employed to shift attention in this scene is to literally change focus in two ways: (1) by going back to the footage that did not make it into the twenty-minute videos and assembling shots in which gal-

Figure 3.2. Close-up on the protagonists.

Figure 3.3. Medium shot with an onlooker.

Figure 3.4. Wide shot showing the gallery.

lery children are clearly visible; and (2) by manipulating the images in the video, using video-editing tools, to shift the center of the frames to the side and the side to the center.

To compose the Madoka video, fourteen hours of video shot over the course of a single day with two cameras were reduced to eighteen minutes, a ratio of less than 3 percent of the footage making it into the final version. The fight scene at Madoka included in the video was reduced from about eighteen minutes of tape to three minutes. That means that there were about fourteen minutes of original footage of this scene we could review to find wider shots as well as close-ups that included *gyarari* children. When we assembled a sequence of the establishing shots from the original video, the *gyarari* children became more visible than they are in most of the close-up shots. Figure 3.5a–d is an example of images that show the participation of *gyarari* children but that were not used in the original twenty-minute tape because in these shots the faces of the fighting boys and the teacher are not clearly visible. These shots, salvaged from the cutting room floor (or, in our

Figure 3.5a–d. Shots of the gallery not used in the twenty-minute edited video.

case, our clip file), can be used to make a new version of the video that tells a different story.

Another technique we have employed to shift the gaze of the viewer is to use tools in our editing software to literally reframe the fight scene. The software allows us to shift the center of shots, moving what was in the center to one side of the frame and what was on one side of the frame to the center. For example, to reframe figure 3.6a, we moved the teacher's face from the center to the right edge of the frame, and Takeshi, watching from the left side of the frame, toward the center (figure 3.6b). A problem with this strategy is that when, as is often the case, the gallery is all around the fights, to shift the image to one side or the other would eliminate half the gallery. One solution is to put the two versions of this picture side by side, one image with the *gyarari* child on the periphery, the other recentered and zoomed in on a *gyarari* child (Figure 3.7a and b).

Another useful approach is to split the screen into two or three, producing a diptych or triptych, which decenters the gaze by giving viewers choices of whom to focus on. When we divide the screen in thirds, the children on

Figure 3.6a and b. Takeshi on periphery and featured.

Figure 3.7a and b. Sakura on periphery and in close-up.

the left and right sides are given their own fields in which to operate. We use this technique to focus attention in the right panel of figure 3.8a and b on Daisuke's head pat while the left panel shows the action of the teacher he is imitating. Figure 3.9a–c is a triptych with the middle panel featuring the teacher and the outer panels featuring the concerned expressions of Takeshi (left panel) and Masa (right panel).

Another strategy is to use the video editing software to reframe and produce a movie segment within a segment, featuring a child who was on the periphery. For example, we have made a twenty-second segment that begins with Masa, in the back corner of the room, struggling to put on his shirt right-side out, noticing the teacher and boys beginning their interaction, and coming close to see what's going on, all the while struggling with his shirt. We can represent the motion of the sequence with a series of still images (figure 3.10a–d).

At one point as Kaizuka talks with the two boys about their fight, a watch-

Figure 3.8a and b. Daisuke imitates the teacher's head pat.

Figure 3.9a–c. Triptych of Takeshi, teacher, and Masa.

Figure 3.10a–d. Masa (in underpants, tracked by blue arrow) approaches the protagonists.

Figure 3.11. Hiroto gives a friendly pat.

Figure 3.12. An imitative head tap from Daisuke.

ing boy reaches over and pats Nobu (figure 3.11), who is teary eyed, on the back. When Kaizuka says to the boys, "God, too, is watching," while she pats Nobu's head for emphasis, Daisuke imitates Kaizuka's action, not quite making contact with Nobu's head (figure 3.12).

FIGHTING AS PERFORMANCE

We can do a similar reanalysis of the teddy bear fight, switching the focus of our attention from the fighting girls to the children who gather around the fight, sometimes just watching and listening, occasionally commenting or reaching in to offer an encouraging pat on the back. As Seiko, Reiko, and Nao fight over the bear, Maki, who throughout the day has been kind to Nao, hovers nearby, at first watching the fighting and then getting a bit involved, putting in her hand for a moment when the three girls are pulling and tugging on a teddy bear (figure 3.13a and b). Maki steps back and watches when the girls' fighting escalates, and they end up in a pile on the floor. At the end of the scramble on the floor, the other girls succeed in wrestling the bear away from Nao.

Nao, having lost control of the teddy bear, starts to cry, and Maki comes over to Nao and touches her comfortingly. In an apparent attempt to mediate the dispute, Maki bends down to talk with Seiko, who is hiding under the table to keep the teddy bear away from Nao (figure 3.14). Maki convinces Seiko to come out and discuss the situation with Nao. Yoko approaches to join the discussion and admonishes Nao for her behavior, telling her not to grab the bear when someone else has it first (figure 3.15).

As Yoko is addressing Nao, Toshi steps into the frame, watches and lis-

Figure 3.13a and b. As the girls fight, Maki watches, concerned, and then reaches in to help Nao.

Figure 3.14. Maki talks to Seiko.   Figure 3.15. Yoko admonishes Nao.

tens for a bit and then puts his hand on Nao's back (figure 3.16). The teddy bear fight concludes with Nao and Seiko interlocking little fingers and sing-ing a song about being friends ("Keep this promise or swallow a thousand needles") (figure 3.17).

When we went back to the original footage from this day that didn't make it into the twenty-minute video, we noticed something we had missed be-fore. Ten minutes or so after the pinkie-shake resolution of the teddy bear fight, Morita calls out that it is cleanup time and the girls return their teddy bears to the storage bin. We then see Maki, who has been watching closely, retrieve from the bin the bear that Nao and Reiko fought over, and walk over and give the bear to Nao, and then lead Nao over to the bin, so that Nao can be the one to last touch and hold the teddy bear before it gets stored away (figure 3.18a–c). We see in Maki's actions here an example of how at a critical juncture a member of the *gyarari* can step out of the role of observer/audi-ence and become a participant in an interaction, adding a coda to the scene and a dimension of empathy that go beyond the pinkie-promise.

Figure 3.16. Toshi, in the dark shirt, looks on.   Figure 3.17. Natsuko watches the pinkie shake.

Figure 3.18a–c. Maki hands the bear to Nao, puts an arm around her, and hugs her.

Several Japanese educators who watched the scene of the teddy bear fight used the word "playing" rather than "fighting" to describe the girls' inter-action. Director Yoshizawa of Komatsudani commented, "It takes a real pro-fessional teacher to tell the difference between a real fight and rough play." A teacher in Tokyo commented: "Basically, they are *jareau* [play fighting]." *Jareau* is most often used for describing the way puppies and kittens engage in mock fights as a way of playing, engaging, and preparing for adulthood.

These comments suggest that experienced Japanese early childhood edu-cators see the children here as playing at fighting rather than fighting. Their comments imply that such play has a performative dimension, a dimension highlighted by Director Kumagai's use of the word *gyarari* to describe the children watching on the periphery of a fight. The children watching are the play's audience and the fighting children the actors. Just as a play needs an audience, such fights need a gallery. In both the hair-pulling and teddy bear fight scenes, the teachers do not tell the children on the periphery to move away, suggesting that they value the participation of the *gyarari*. Japanese early childhood educators' comments on these scenes suggest that the role of the *gyarari* in such fights is complex, and that being a member of such a gallery is a valuable learning opportunity for the children watching as well as a form of social control over the fighting children.

SYMPATHETIC IDENTIFICATION AND
LEGITIMATE PERIPHERAL PARTICIPATION

The word *gallery* seems to suggest that those watching are passive, but this is not how the Japanese educators we interviewed described the *gyarari* that gathered around the fights in the videos. Several teachers emphasized the distinction between active and passive watching by making a distinction between being a member of a *gyarari*, on the one hand, and being a *yajiuma* (onlooker) or *bōkansha* (bystander) on the other (Akiba 2004; Morita and Kiyonaga 1996). The word *yajiuma* is most often used for describing people's behavior at sites of accidents. For instance, people who gather around a car accident out of curiosity and speculate about what happened and who was at fault are called *yajiuma*, which is sometimes translated into English as "rubbernecker."

The word is derogatory, suggesting that those gathering around are motivated not by genuine concern but only by curiosity and a desire for vicarious thrills. One teacher said about the watching children in the video: "They look kind of like *yajiuma*, but not really, because they are worried." This teacher suggests that it is the children's appearance of being worried, implying empathy, which makes them legitimate peripheral participants, rather than mere onlookers. *Bōkansha* (bystander) is a word used in Japan mostly in social psychology, as in the technical term "bystander effect." It is used to refer to people who watch with no intent to be participants. This term, like *yajiuma*, was used by teachers to distinguish illegitimate from legitimate participation, as in the comment of a teacher in Tokyo who said: "Those watching the children involved in the fight are not *bōkansha* [bystanders]. They are people concerned about their friends; they are *all* participants."

Like the audience at a play, the people in the galleries that gather around these fights are potentially both moved and edified by their viewing. Japanese educators emphasized that it is not only the children directly involved who learn from fights and their resolution, but also the children watching, through observational learning and sympathetic identification. Japanese preschool teachers often used the words *kimochi* (feelings), *dōjō* (sympathy), and *omoiyari* (empathy) to describe children's experience of watching their classmates engaged in emotionally intense interactions. As one teacher said, "Sympathizing with others is important."

The experience of the *gyarari*, therefore, can be conceived as a form of vicarious participation, in which the observing children feel (or at least attempt to feel) what is being experienced by a classmate. The behavior of the *gyarari* children in the fighting scenes, as well as Japanese educators' reflections on these scenes, is largely consistent with Lave and Wenger's (1991) concept of "legitimate peripheral participation," and with the related concepts of "observational learning" and "intent participation." Rogoff and her colleagues (2003) describe intent participation as "keenly observing and listening in anticipation of or in the process of engaging in an endeavor" (176). Gaskins and Paradise (2009) write, "Observational learning typically occurs in familiar contexts in which one person performs an activity while another person, who knows less, watches them do it" (85). Lave and Wenger (1991) define legitimate peripheral participation as

> a way to speak about the relations between newcomers and old-timers, and about activities, identities, artifacts, and communities of knowledge and practice. A person's intentions to learn are engaged and the meaning of learning is configured through the process of becoming a full participant in a socio-cultural practice. This social process includes, indeed it subsumes, the learning of knowledgeable skills. (29)

The Japanese practices and beliefs we have presented here are unlike most descriptions in the literature of peripheral participation and observational learning in several key ways. First, the learning here is not, as in most of the studies of peripheral participation and observational learning, of a cognitive skill or a trade, but instead of social skills and emotional dispositions. The children are learning, through observation and sympathetic identification, how to feel, what to do with their feelings, and how to behave as a member of a caring community. Such learning in the domains of emotions and sociality is underdiscussed in the peripheral participation literature, which emphasizes the cognitive and skill domains, but well described in the psychological anthropological literature on enculturation (e.g., by Briggs 1999; Hayashi, Karasawa, and Tobin 2009) and in some conceptualizations of observational learning. For example, Gaskins and Paradise (2009) suggest that children learn culturally structured rules about social behavior and social roles in large part by observing the interactions that go on around them: "They can also observe the consequences of certain social acts in their particular social worlds—what Bandura (1977) called *vicarious reinforcement*—by observing others who share a social category with them and are seen therefore to be 'like me' (e.g., gender, age, race, or class)" (108).

This points to a second key difference between the *gyarari* situations of peer learning we have presented in this chapter, and Lave and Wenger's notion of legitimate peripheral participation and Rogoff and her collaborators' notion of intent participation, which emphasize learning in hierarchical rather than peer contexts, and most often describing those observing and those being observed as "newcomers and old-timers" or as "masters and apprentices." We are not suggesting that such hierarchical forms of peripheral participation are not important in Japan, which is well known for its rich traditions of apprenticeship learning in the arts (Singleton 1998), or that hierarchical learning is a form of peripheral participation not found in Japanese preschools. Both the original and the new *Preschool in Three Cultures* books describe the importance that teachers at Komatsudani and other Japanese preschools give to the benefits of mixed-age learning (*tate-wari kyōiku*) for both the younger and the older children (Tobin, Wu, and Davidson 1989; Tobin, Hsueh, and Karasawa 2009; Ben-Ari 1996). But alongside the value placed on learning from old-timers, in Japanese preschools there is also a great emphasis placed on the value and importance of learning through peer relationships. "Peer" is a relative term. Even in classes of children of the same grade, there are differences of age and experience. Nao is the youngest and newest child in her class, and her teacher suggested this played a role in the girls' behaviors during the teddy bear fight. But according to Morita and other Japanese teachers, the underlying value of allowing the children to experience fighting and emotions, both directly and vicariously, is that the children interact as a community of peers.

The third distinction we want to emphasize, which is the focus of the section that follows, is that whereas most of Lave and Wenger's examples are of people learning as individuals, the *gyarari* situations emphasize group learning and group experience. None of these points are inherently inconsistent with Lave and Wenger's conceptualization of legitimate peripheral participation, Gaskin and Paradise's of observational learning, and Rogoff and her colleagues' of intent participation. Each of these theories is implicitly concerned with social as well as cognitive learning, in that peripheral participation and intent participation function not only to learn skills, but also to help individuals become full, appropriate, contributing members of a community (Singleton 1998). Our argument is that the Japanese emic view can deepen the concepts of peripheral participation and intent participation by adding more explicit emphasis on the acquisition of social-emotional skills, on learning with and from peers, and on peripherally participating as a group.

THE GALLERY'S EMBODIED ENGAGEMENT

In his 1996 article on naptime in Japanese nursery schools, Eyal Ben-Ari uses ideas by Abu-Lughod and Lutz (1990) on the embodiment of emotion to demonstrate how Japanese young children transfer forms of emotional exchange learned at home with their family members to their interactions with their classmates in preschool. Ben-Ari focuses on the multisensorial experience of co-sleeping. A similar case can be made for the embodiment of emotion in children's fights at preschool. For the children fighting, the teddy bear scuffle was clearly embodied, not just because of the bodily contact, but also because of the intense shared experiencing of the sights, sounds, kinesthesia, and smells that accompany rolling around on the floor, pulling on a bear, the interlocking of pinkies while making a promise, the wiping away of tears, and the embrace at the fight's resolution. What is less readily apparent is how the fight provides an experience of embodied learning of emotions not only for the fights' protagonists, but also for those gathered on the periphery, who also engage multisensorially with the action. Rather than being passive, the *gyarari* children are engaged in intense, focused looking and listening and even, at times, in reaching out and touching the fight protagonists. Moreover, unlike a member of a theater audience who is generally confined to a single seat at some remove from the action on the stage, the members of the *gyarari* at these fights move around, sometimes approaching close enough to touch the protagonists, sometimes moving back, and sometimes imitating with their bodies the protagonists' movements.

COLLECTIVE VS. SELF REGULATION

Most U.S. early childhood educational practices and beliefs, as well as Western theories of child development, conceptualize constraint on antisocial behavior as self-constraint. In contrast, Japanese early childhood educators' reflections on the two *gyarari* scenes emphasize the importance for children of learning to function as a self-monitoring, self-controlling community. The locus of control on misbehavior is in the group, rather than in each child as an individual. Japanese early childhood educators conceive the *gyarari* not as a gaggle of busybodies, but rather as a collective, with the power to induce prosocial and limit antisocial behavior in others.

When we asked preschool teachers if they ever tell children who are watching fights to move away, most said no and emphasized that this sort of participation was beneficial not just for the watching children, but also for those being watched. For example, a teacher in Tokyo answered, "Most of the times, I tell the children who are directly involved that other children care about you and are worried about you." In addition to providing empathy and emotional support, the observing children are seen as a moderating influence on the fight protagonists. As Professor Hiroshi Usui said about the teddy bear fight scene: "The watching children function as one of the factors that control fighting. The observers don't let the stronger children take things away from the weaker ones. They provide some self-regulation to the fighters." Professor Usui's comment expresses the Japanese cultural belief in the collective ability of the group to self-regulate and in the importance of preschool as a site for this collective ability to be experienced, learned, practiced, and cultivated.

Rather than passive observers, the children watching in these fight scenes are active on several levels. They are active in the sense that they choose to watch and to attend to what they are watching. They are active also in the sense that they respond to the actions they are observing. Some of the watching children literally take action, closing the gap between actors and audience, protagonists and observers. For example, Yoko is among the peripherally involved children watching the teddy bear fight until Reiko says to her, "You should scold her [Nao]." Yoko responds to this call and abandons her spot in the *gyarari* to become an actor. As Yoko admonishes Nao, she puts her arm around her waist, as if playing the part of a teacher or mother. In the Madoka video we see Daisuke, a boy in the *gyarari*, become physically involved when he reaches out and pats one of the disputants on the head, mimicking a gesture just made by the teacher.

Director Machiyama referred to the children on the periphery of the fight at Madoka not as a *gyarari*, but as a *gaiya*: "The *gaiya* choose to watch their friends' fights." *Gaiya* is a word used in Japan mostly in baseball, where it can mean the fans seated in the bleachers, and in this sense the meaning is close to that of the word *gyarari*. But it can also mean the outfielders. The outfielders spend most of the game standing some distance from the central action, but their active participation, though sporadic, is essential. The children on the periphery of the fights are, to follow Director Machiyama's metaphor, both like fans in the bleachers cheering on their team and like outfielders, watching and waiting, ready to make a play when needed.

For most contemporary children, in Japan as in many other countries, preschool provides their first opportunity to learn to be a member of a community. Japanese preschools are sites for teaching young children to have a characteristically Japanese sense of self, which is to say a sense of self that is socially minded. Japanese educators' notions of peripheral participation in fights is a piece of this larger picture of how Japanese preschool classrooms function as sites for teaching young children to develop a collective as well as individual sense of self and of social responsibility.

The concept of collective self-regulation sounds oxymoronic to Western ears, but not so in Japan. The belief of Japanese educators that the locus of control for fighting and other antisocial behaviors is at the level of the group rather than the individual is a useful challenge to Western psychological theories of self-regulation and more generally of child development (Shimizu 2000). Most of the psychological work on the development of prosociality focuses on how individual children experience and express emotions and control or fail to control their behavior. Eisenberg and Spinrad (2004) make a useful distinction between self-regulation and externally imposed regulation, and "between being able to regulate emotion oneself and modulating emotion primarily through the efforts of others" (336). A Japanese emic perspective would recast this distinction as that between a group regulated by its own emotions and behaviors and one regulated by others (e.g., by the teacher).

This Japanese perspective on behavioral regulation, while not discounting the importance of individual processes of emotion, cognition, and behavior, would expand the Western psychological literature by seeing the preschool classroom as controlled not just or primarily by the sum of the self-regulation abilities of each child, but also by the collective emotional and social skills of the class. The focus is on helping children learn to be members of the class as a community, and then on providing opportunities for this community to develop the capacity to self-regulate.

In arguing that the Japanese emic understanding of peripheral participation emphasizes the encouragement of a collective locus of control, we do not mean to suggest that peripherally participating Japanese children do not also have individual motives or that they lack the ability for self-control. As Raeff (2000; 2006) argues, it cannot be the case that children in some cultures are entirely independent and in some cultures interdependent, for all cultures require people to act both independently and interdependently. Therefore the focus of our analysis should be on explicating in which contexts in a culture children are expected to act independently and in which contexts interdependently. We are suggesting not that Japanese teachers always or consistently discourage independence, but that in the domain of dealing with children's fights in Japanese preschool classrooms, there is general encouragement from teachers for an interdependent solution.

IJIME

Many U.S. educators who watched the scene of the teddy bear fight at Komatsudani suggested that Nao was the victim here of bullying from the group of girls. However, none of the Japanese early childhood educators we interviewed offered this interpretation. In contemporary Japan, bullying (*ijime*) is considered to be a significant educational and social problem (Akiba 2004), especially at the middle school level (LeTendre 2000; Fukuzawa and LeTendre 2001). *Ijime* in its paradigmatic form involves a group of children, or even a whole class, ostracizing, teasing, and in other ways harassing a single child. Akiba (2004) suggests that *ijime* should be viewed as both an effect and a symptom of a more general breakdown of society, a form of Japanese postmodern anomie in which the traditional community structures have been eroded:

> With a smaller number of businessmen spending after hours for socializing with their colleagues and a diminished sense of local community where neighbors are strangers, it is becoming more difficult to expect their children to develop group-orientation and trusting peer

relationships. Despite these societal changes, there have been few changes in the school organization to foster collective values to prepare students for society. The impact of the gap between the societal changes and the traditional role of schools to foster Japanese cultural values needs to be examined in relation to *ijime* phenomenon in future studies. (234)

While *ijime* is mostly a middle-school and high-school phenomenon, Japanese educators are concerned about the antecedents in lower grades. Some Japanese educators we interviewed (but none of the early childhood educators) saw in the fight over the teddy bear at Komatsudani the beginnings of *ijime*. For example, Masakazu Mitsumura, who studies middle-school *ijime*, said of the girls' fight:

> In my opinion, what we see happening in this scene in your video might contribute to the development of *ijime* behavior later. I worry less about the children directly involved in the fight than about the effect on the bystanders, who are watching and developing bad habits of following the lead of the dominant figures in the classroom and becoming passive bullies.

In contrast, the Japanese early childhood educators we interviewed, while agreeing that *ijime* is a major social concern and that the antecedents of classroom behavior and misbehavior begin in preschool, argued that the social skills children need to acquire to cohere as an effective classroom community are best supported not through direct instruction or heavy teacher intervention, but instead by providing ample opportunities for young children collectively to experience complex social interactions. As Morita explained:

> If I think that a fight, such as this one in the video, is unlikely to result in anybody getting hurt, I stay back and wait and observe. I want the children to learn to be strong enough to handle such small quarrels. I want them to have the power to endure. If it's not dangerous, I welcome their fighting.

When we asked Morita to respond to the suggestion that the girls were bullying Nao, she replied:

She is strong. All the children have strong personalities, so in this kind of situation they all want to make their case and put forward their opinion. Compared with the other children, Nao is not very good at speaking. She cries when she can't express what she wants to say verbally. But as you saw in the video, even while she was crying, Nao tried to pull the teddy bear back. She has a strong core.

Morita went on to explain that she viewed Nao's behavior, though babyish, as prosocial, a view she had as well of the older girls' aggressive responses. *Ijime* usually takes the form of ostracizing and excluding a classmate seen as weak. Nao's interactions with the other girls are just the opposite: intense emotional interactions, initiated by Nao as well as her classmates, with the expression of affection as well as anger and critique. In this sense we suggest that the fighting scenes we are analyzing here are the precursors not of middle-school *ijime*, but of the opposite—the kind of rich social interactions that allow young children to learn to experience themselves as members of a classroom community and collectively regulate their behavior.

SEKEN NO ME: THE SOCIAL GAZE

As she is mediating the hair-pulling fight, Kaizuka says to the two boys: "Kamisama datte miterun dayo." In English this can be translated as either "God, too, is watching," "The gods, too, are watching," or "The spirits, too, are watching you." The notion of god in Shinto comes from the belief that everything in nature—water, mountains, flowers, trees, rocks—have spirits and therefore are kinds of gods. There is a Shinto expression that refers to "eight million spirits," which implies that the eyes of the gods are everywhere. We see a connection between this Shinto notion and the cultural concept of *seken no me*. *Seken* literally means "society"; *me* means "eyes." Together, they mean literally, "the eyes of society," or, following Takie Lebra's (1976) definition, "the generalized audience." Lebra lists a set of related terms: *seken-nami* (conforming to *seken* standards, or ordinary), *seken-banare* (incongruent with *seken* conventions, or eccentric), and *seken-shirazu* (unaware of *seken* rules, or naïve). Like Kaizuka's phrase "The gods, too, are watching," *seken no me* carries the meaning of being aware that one is always being watched. A related phrase used by many of the Japanese early childhood educators to describe the children on the periphery of the fight scenes was *mawari no ko*, literally, "the children around" or "the surrounding children." This phrase was sometimes used in conjunction with *mawari no iken*—the opinions of the people around you.

Interestingly, Kaizuka said not just, "The gods [*kamisama*] are watching," but "The gods, *too*, are watching." *Datte* means "as well" or "too." Who else, then, besides the gods, is watching the boys? One interpretation is that their teacher, Kaizuka is also always watching. Another interpretation is that everyone in the community of the classroom is always watching each other (an interpretation that is a paraphrase of *seken no me*, or "generalized audience"). We therefore interpret the comment "The gods, too, are watching" as Kaizuka's way of reminding the boys and the surrounding *gyarari* of the existence of people around them, who are watching and care about them.

As mentioned in chapter 1, in earlier times everyone in a Japanese village or city neighborhood took responsibility for watching and correcting children. Such collective regulation of behavior has become less common in modern Japan, where demographic change and modernization has led to the dissolution of traditional rural and urban neighborhoods and therefore of the power of the *seken* (generalized others) and *mawari no iken* (opinions of others). With this shift, preschools have increasingly become the first and most important place where young children come to practice and experience being watched by and watching others. Professor Hiroshi Usui told us that he approved of teachers' giving children opportunities to solve their own disputes because it allows children to experience a social complexity lacking in their lives at home:

> This is compensatory education. These days, children lack opportunities to experience human relationships. In the old days, children had siblings, but not anymore. Now that Japan is wealthy, children have their own toys and own rooms. Living this way, they never have the experience of fighting over toys and other things, and of watching others fight.

A preschool director in Tokyo said of the children's desire to be part of the *gyarari* watching the fights: "There is nothing that is not their business. Everything that happens here is everybody's business when they are at the preschool. They live together."

The value Japanese educators place on the socializing power of the gaze of others contrasts with Foucault's notion of panopticism, and more generally with discourses in Western scholarship on visibility and power. In Western educational discourse, it is the teacher, with eyes in the back of her head, trained in the importance of setting up her classroom so all her students are always visible to her, whose gaze maintains classroom order. In contrast, in the Japanese early childhood classroom, it is the group of children who are encouraged to keep each other in view and to use their collective gaze to maintain order. In such a classroom, power is more diffuse, not concentrated in the teacher.

In *Discipline and Punish* (1977), Foucault discusses the operation of the Panopticon, the prison invented in the eighteenth century by Jeremy Bentham, in which a single guard peering out through a small window can survey and thereby control a hundred or more prisoners housed in a grid of cells. But for Foucault the more chillingly effective form of surveillance is the internalization of the Panopticon and the rise of the self-monitoring, self-judging, self-punishing modern ego. In contemporary Western society, this inward disciplinary gaze is created in the child both at home and also in the preschool, where the goal is that he eventually will not need to be watched by others and will learn to watch himself. The discourse of Japanese early childhood education emphasizes neither control of misbehavior by the surveillance of the teacher (the Panopticon model), nor control through the self-regulation of the individual members of the class (the internalization model), but instead control through collective responsibility and collective surveillance and vigilance. In this model the gaze is the gaze of a gallery, not of a guard in a tower. And the gaze is seen as primarily prosocial and humanizing, rather than as draconian and dehumanizing.

Most writing on *seken* emphasizes the positive effect this generalizing gaze has on potential or actual miscreants, whose impulse to misbehave is controlled by fear of public censure and shame. But we suggest that the experience of being part of a *seken* and sharing in administering the collective gaze is also beneficial for the gazers, who have an opportunity to participate in intense emotional experiences and to experience the sense of community such shared participation produces in all involved.

PROVIDING OPPORTUNITIES FOR PERIPHERAL PARTICIPATION

This implicit cultural practice of not intervening in children's disputes does not mean never intervening, but instead having nonintervention in children's fights as an option, a strategy teachers can deploy. In the Komatsudani video, Morita chooses not to intervene as the girls fight over the bear. In the Madoka video, in contrast, we see Kaizuka intervene much more aggressively in the dispute between the two boys, which she ended up mediating. By pulling back our focus, and attending not to the children who were the protagonists in the fight, but instead to the children on the periphery, we can see how in these dissimilar interactions these teachers in different ways created an opportunity for a *gyarari* to form and for a group of children to experience vicarious emotion, empathize, and learn.

As we discuss in chapter 1, for a teacher to make a strategy of *mimamoru* effective, children need to know she is paying enough attention to give them confidence that someone will be there to keep things from getting totally out of control, but the teachers' presence, her watchfulness, has to be soft enough so children take responsibility and perform primarily not for her but rather for and in interaction with their classmates. In their review of observational learning Gaskins and Paradise (2009) emphasize that when children are allowed to follow their interests and are given only minimal feedback, "they take initiative in directing their attention and finding or creating activities to practice on their own skills they have not yet mastered" (97). By avoiding being the primary audience for the children's performance, Morita allows for a child-oriented, childlike piece of drama to unfold.

While Kaizuka's interventionist approach seems to be the opposite of Morita's, there is a deeper similarity. Kaizuka intervenes with the fighting boys, but not with the *gyarari* who gathers around them. Both teachers allow children on the periphery of these fights to take on the roles of the audience, of the legitimate peripherally participating classroom community.

We are not suggesting that it is at all unusual for children in countries other than Japan to become peripheral participants in fights. What we are suggesting is that the way Japanese teachers respond to such fights and to the role of those peripherally involved is characteristically Japanese. In Chapter 2 we argued that the cultural practice of Japanese preschool teachers emphasizes allowing the fighting children to experience a range of emotions and to benefit from the opportunity to work out their own solutions to disputes. In this chapter we have expanded this analysis by adding that the Japanese teachers' goal is to encourage not just the protagonists at the center of the fight but also the wider group of children who gather around fights to explore, collectively, childlike solutions to disputes. Rather than telling the galleries of peripherally participating children "Move away" or "This is none of your business," Japanese teachers allow and quietly encourage children to get involved in everything that goes on in the classroom.

In closing, we would add that although our focus in this chapter has been on the *gyarari* that forms around fights, Japanese early childhood educators are also supportive of peripheral participation of children in other emotion-laden events, such as experiencing sadness, as we described in chapter 2. Fights are dramatic, but they are far from the only dramas that take place every day in preschool classrooms.

Chapter 4

—

Learning Embodied Culture

Figure 4.1.

THE ACCIDENTAL PUNCH

There is a thirty-second scene in the Komatsudani video where a four-year-old boy, Toshi, accidentally hits a girl, Maki, in the chest as he carelessly, but not maliciously, swings his arms, as if he is engaging with her in a mock fight. Toshi immediately says "Gomen" (sorry) to Maki and does a short bow. Not accepting Toshi's apology, Maki instead theatrically exaggerates how much he has hurt her by clasping the spot on her chest with both hands and then bending over a table in apparent pain. A classmate, Toru, who has been watching the interaction, rushes over to help, patting Maki on the back and suggesting that she tell the teacher (which she does not do). Toshi comes over and attempts to mollify Maki by repeatedly saying "Gomen" as he leans in toward her, finally laying his torso on the table, in a position mirroring Maki's. Maki finally seems to accept Toshi's apology, and she gets up and walks away.

We suggest that this apparently straightforward preschool classroom interaction merits deeper analysis, as it features complex displays of embodied actions. Why did Toshi's repeated verbal apologies and his initial bows fail to mollify Maki? Why did his bows at the end of the interaction have a more positive effect? In this chapter we provide microanalyses of this and other scenes from our videos that show Japanese children using culturally patterned techniques bodily, sometimes awkwardly, sometimes fluently, to deal with social interactions.

The core argument of this chapter, and indeed one of the main points we develop in this book, is that cultures are composed not only of beliefs, values, and ways of thinking and feeling, but also of corporeal practices. Characteristically Japanese corporeal practices include taking off shoes to enter a room, sitting on the floor on tatami mats, eating with chopsticks, and bowing. In this chapter we explore how these and other techniques of the body are learned in Japanese preschools, and more generally how preschools function as key sites for the enculturation not only of speech and thought, but also of bodies. Japanese preschools are places where Japanese young children learn to move, use, and position their bodies in characteristically Japanese ways and therefore, in a crucial sense, where they become Japanese.

Although in this chapter we feature analyses of bodily techniques of children, as in the other chapters our central concern is on Japanese preschool teachers' pedagogical practices. The pedagogical practices we examine in this chapter are those used by Japanese preschool teachers to support the development in children of culturally normative bodily techniques. Compared with the earlier chapters, this chapter features fewer analyses of quotes from teachers and more microanalyses of still images exported from the videos.

In the introduction we cited Pascal's argument that you do not pray because you are religious; you are religious because you pray. In other words, the bodily action precedes rather than follows the belief. This is the core logic of this chapter, in which we argue: "You don't bow because you are Japanese. You are Japanese because you bow." Our goal is to present the core bodily techniques of Japanese culture that children master in Japanese preschools, techniques, we argue, that make them Japanese.

We find Bakhtin's notions of citationality, discourse, and dialogism useful for thinking about children's embodied interactions. Bakhtin for the most part wrote not about bodies but about words. His central concern was with how words are inherently heteroglossic, dialogic, and citational, with the meaning of an utterance determined by contexts of use and intertextual associations, rather than by the intentions of the author/speaker. We suggest that we can apply Bakhtinian conceptions of language to bodily techniques. Doing so suggests some neologisms, bodily versions of his logocentric concepts: heteroglossic becomes heterocorporeal; polyvocal becomes polycorporeal; intertextual becomes intercorporeal. For other key concepts we just need to add "body" to balance the implied foregrounding of words: *bodily* answerability ("we answer with our *bodies*"); forms of *bodily* mimesis, parody, and inflection/attitude (these are discussed in *Rabelais and His World*); *bodily* versions of direct and indirect quotation; *bodily* authoritative and internally persuasive techniques. Bakhtin (1982) suggests that "the word in language is half someone else's" (294.) We would add that this is true as well for the movements of bodies. Preschool children observe, cite, and sometimes parody the movements of their teachers and peers in the process of what Bakhtin calls their ideological becoming. Because bodily movements, like utterances, require not just models to cite but also the response of another to have meaning, preschool children must learn to enter into bodily dialogues, rather than monologues, and to answer the movements of the other.

CONTEXTS AND *KEJIME*

This chapter is concerned not just with how Japanese preschool children master techniques of the body, but also with how they learn to match these bodily techniques to the contexts they encounter in their everyday lives in preschool. In all cultures, people are expected to adjust their behavior to contexts, but not all cultures mark contexts as explicitly as is the case in Japan, or require such dramatic shifts in comportment. As Nancy Rosenberger (1989) writes about Japanese culture: "Central to movement among modes of self is the principle of contextualization; by moving among contexts, Japanese can shift among modes of self-presentation. Contexts can change according to place, time, and/or social group" (99).

Stereotypical views by outsiders often depict Japan, erroneously, as a formal culture. It is true that when interacting with outsiders, with guests, in business meetings, and in other formal situations, Japanese employ formal speech and bodily registers. But when interacting with insiders and in informal situations, Japanese employ informal registers, both linguistically and with their bodies. What is characteristic of Japanese culture is not formality but alterations of conduct in different situations: in formal and informal contexts; with insiders and with outsiders; in different places (temples vs. baths); in different parts of the same place (front vs. rear doors of houses); and at different times (the ceremonies that open and close events vs. during the events themselves).

There is a Japanese term for matching comportment to context. *Kejime o tsukeru* means "to draw a line between two situations," "to make distinctions," or "to act in a way appropriate to the context." Perhaps the closest phrase we have in today's English is "good manners." Good manners require children to identify the context, know what words and bodily movements are appropriate to that context, and then use the appropriate words and movements. Japanese preschools present young children with a variety of temporal, spatial, and situational contexts, calling for a variety of language registers and modes of bodily comportment.

Contexts are spatial. Entering a home, temple building, or traditional restaurant in Japan is marked by the removal of shoes and a bow. In all three preschools where we videotaped, we have shots of children removing their shoes in the *genkan* (entrance way/entrance hall) of the building, and shots of teachers, parents, and children bowing to greet each other. At Madoka and many other kindergartens, children not only change their shoes in the *genkan* (figure 4.2a and b), but also change their uniforms when they enter their classroom (figure 4.3). The school or classroom entranceway marks a divide not only between a literal inside and outside, but also between children's sense of being at home and being at preschool and between the comportments each of these contexts requires.

Contexts are also temporal. Changes in seasons are clearly defined in Japan, with, for example, summer ending and fall beginning on October 1. This date marks a series of transitions including a change from summer to fall clothing and a change from chilled to warm tea. The preschool curriculum follows this seasonal variation, with changes in school decorations and uniforms and an emphasis on the observances of holidays, such as the sports festival in May and the rice-planting festival in June, occasions that call for both more formal and more informal bodily comportment than usual.

Contexts are also relational. When addressing someone younger, different language and posture are used from those for addressing one's senior. We see this in the meetings in the teachers lounge before the schoolday begins and during the structured mixed-age activity at Komatsudani, where older children each day go to the nursery to help care for the babies and toddlers.

Figure 4.2a and b. *Genkan* and changing shoes.

Figure 4.3. Changing clothes.

Among age mates, role and status differences come into play during periods of the day when some children take on the role of *tōban* (class monitor).

PEDAGOGIES OF EMBODIMENT

In chapter 2, we described how Japanese preschool teachers emphasize the role of embodied experiences (*taiken*) in the development of emotions and social skills. The same logic underlies the approach Japanese preschool teachers take to supporting the development in children of appropriate comportment and techniques of the body. In our interviews, teachers emphasized that the most effective way to help children develop appropriate bodily techniques is to give them repeated, abundant, and varied opportunities to practice adjusting their embodied behavior to changing contexts.

A thesis of this chapter is that one of the core goals of the Japanese preschool is for children to learn *kejime*, to adjust their behavior according to changing contexts. And yet in our observations we never heard a teacher use the term *kejime* with her students or talk in an abstract way about the need to adjust behavior to contexts. Instead, we suggest, *kejime* is taught implicitly, by structuring the preschool's architecture, routines, and curriculum so as to assure that children experience a range of contexts, and so as to make it easy and attractive for them to join teachers and classmates in performing the forms of speech and bodily comportment appropriate to the changing contexts of the Japanese schoolday (Ben-Ari 1997). The Japanese preschool presents enough variety of social interactions and contexts to provide children with multiple opportunities to practice a range of techniques of the body and to learn to read contexts accurately and to know when a shift in context calls for a shift of levels of behavior. As Kaizuka explained:

> At the beginning of their preschool life, children usually don't listen when I talk. But over time, when I say, "I would like to talk," they start to look at me. For example, they gradually come to know that they need to listen to me during morning opening. Shifting one's behavior when a new activity starts is part of learning *kejime*. I believe that *kejime* is important. If there were no *kejime*, then the life of preschool would be borderless [*daradara*]. It's important to be formal [*kichinto*] when needed, like during morning opening. But then, when it's time to play, children should play, in a childlike way.

At Madoka, as at the majority of yōchien, children wear a formal uniform for ceremonies and for going to and from school and an informal uniform (gym shorts and a t-shirt) while at school. When we asked why the children change uniforms, Director Machiyama told us:

> It's important to change clothes. It makes children realize the time and place where they are. It's good to have uniforms because children can change their mood from casual to formal when they put on uniforms.

The verb Machiyama uses here for changing from a casual to formal mood is *hikishimeru*, which literally means "to stiffen," a denotation that carries the suggestion that the change in emotional mood that accompanies a change into uniform is accompanied by a change in posture (a straightening of the back).

In each of our videos we see teachers lead their students in bowing during the morning gathering, pre-meal ceremony, and end of the day farewells. When it is time for these group activities, the teacher cues the children either by changing her location and demeanor, or verbally (or, in the case of Meisei School for the Deaf, by flashing the lights). These actions cue the children to the need to change their demeanor from the bodily attitude of free play to the comportment expected for participation in a structured group activity. In these situations teachers communicate expectations, but rarely use pressure. As Director Kumagai of Senzan Yōchien, told us:

> When they arrive at school, children put away their bags and then go outside to play freely. Then when morning exercise starts, the children come together. There are some children who do not come on their own, but we don't bring them over. In this situation we don't tell them to line up, because it's not their behavior that needs to change, but their heart and mind [kokoro]. They have to *want* to come together. This is very important. If we say, "You need to line up," it doesn't have any meaning, because they would be doing it only because we are telling them to do so.

Director Kumagai suggests, and many of our other informants concur, that compelling children to participate in structured activities is counterproductive. Instead, as Ben-Ari (1997) and Peak (1991) have argued, the approach taken in most Japanese preschools is to make children *want* to participate. Under this approach, some children spontaneously join the morning exercise and others do not; some bow a morning greeting, while others do not; some bow deeply, while others make just a slight nod; and some put hands together before the pre-meal greeting (figure 4.4a and b), and others do not. Even those children who do not perform the bodily routines of these ceremonial interludes that punctuate the day are included in the group by virtue of not being identified as misbehaving, resisting, or failing. While not moving their bodies in unison with their classmates, they are still included as legitimate peripheral participants.

On one of our return visits to Senzan Yōchien, at the end of the schoolday, we saw one of the younger teachers, Takeshi Yamada (who was the only male

Figure 4.4a and b. Putting hands together before saying "Itadakimasu."

teacher at the school), bowing to each of the children in his class in the gate area where their mothers picked them up. We later asked Yamada to comment on a photo we took of one of these bows:

Figure 4.5. Yamada bows deeply to a departing child.

> HAYASHI: We took this picture of you at the gate (figure 4.5).
>
> YAMADA: Hmmm. Modeling. Between this child and me. Here [pointing to the left side of the photo] it's *yōchien*. From here [pointing to right side of photo] it's home. This [pointing to the middle] is the border between home and school, the place where we say "Good morning" and "Goodbye."
>
> TOBIN: Why the bow?
>
> YAMADA: For greeting. There is a phrase we have written on the school gate: "One greeting, one heart." There is a well-known phrase, "One meeting, one life." This means that we should appreciate even a single occasion of meeting someone. Senzan's saying comes from this idea. We want children to greet each other. If we greet children, children greet us back.

TOBIN: The greeting we see you doing here in the picture looks
very polite. Usually when people who know each other greet each
other, there isn't such a polite bow, right?

YAMADA: Hmm. I also do this kind of deep bow at bus stops, when I
ride the bus to pick up children.

TOBIN: To whom are you bowing?

YAMADA: Mothers, children, teachers.

HAYASHI: When there are only mothers present, do you change the
way you bow?

YAMADA: Yes. I bow deeper to children than I do to adults, where I
usually just [demonstrating a slight bowing, nodding of the head]
while saying "Good morning."

We showed the picture of Yamada's deep bow to Director Kumagai:

TOBIN: Yamada did a deep bow here. Why does he bow so deeply?

KUMAGAI: He's being a model. He believes that children watch the
way he does things. Just [bowing slightly] doesn't get through to
children.

TOBIN: So the bow is for children, not mothers.

KUMAGAI: I don't think Yamada-sensei does such deep bows to
mothers. He does deep bows to children because he thinks that
this is an important point in children's life for developing this
practice.

BOWING IN TWO PLANES

The bow is the most characteristically Japanese of bodily positions. Japanese
people bow in a variety of situations, for a variety of reasons, in a variety
of ways. People bow to greet each other on the street, to show gratitude,
respect, or apology. In conversations, people bow subtly to indicate agreement, to acknowledge that they are listening or that they are thinking about
what someone has said to them. Learning how to bow is not only about
learning how to bend one's back, shoulders, and head in synchrony, but also
about learning when to bow, and just how far to bend for each bowing context, from a deep bow in front of a temple altar or person of status from
whom one wants a favor, to a slight nodding, dipping motion when greeting

a friend. Other variations include the hand position during the bow, with hands on thighs, clasped in front at the waist, or held behind one's back. This modulation of bowing and of other bodily techniques is based on context, on the time and space of interactions in combination with the genders, statuses, personalities, and moods of the people interacting.

Modulations in the formality of a bow depending on the context are the corporeal equivalents of the shifts in register that are a characteristic feature of spoken Japanese, along a continuum that runs from the *keigo* ("respectful" or "honorific" language) used in formal and ceremonial situations, to the polite form of speech (*teineigo*) used in everyday business and social interactions, to the plain form (*kudaketa*) used in the home and among friends. Other languages, including English, have different speech registers for different contexts, but these speech registers are not as explicitly or formally marked as they are in Japanese. We are suggesting that this is the case as well with Japanese bodily techniques, which, like Japanese speech, have distinct registers.

Our microanalyses of the bodily movements of children and teachers in the videos have led us to a hypothesis: bowing and other movements in the vertical plane are more associated with formality, and tilting and other movements in the horizontal plane with informality. Such vertical movements as a downward nod of the chin, bowing of the head, and bowing of the whole body characterize the formal bodily register. The informal bodily register, in contrast, is characterized by horizontal movements, from a slight tilting of the head to the right or left, to a swaying back and forth of the upper torso. The vertical movements are crisper, almost military, in contrast to the more relaxed, less regimented movements in the horizontal plane (figures 4.6–9).

For example, in the formal portion of the morning staff meeting the teachers and directors stand straight (figure 4.10a) and move stiffly, mostly in the vertical plane, punctuating each other's utterances with nods and short bows and beginning and ending the meeting with deep bows (figure 4.10b). In contrast, during the informal talk in the staff room the teachers make some vertical movements, in the form of nods of the head and leaning the torso forward and back, but these vertical movements are relaxed and imprecise (figure 4.10c). Most of the teachers' movements in these informal conversational contexts leave the vertical plane, as they combine nods of agreement with tilts of the face and body to indicate engagement in the conversation and agreement and, less often, disagreement with what is being said.

Figure 4.11a–c shows a range of formal versions of bowing, from teachers and children bowing to greet each other as they arrive at school, to bowing while saying *itadakimasu* (the pre-meal greeting) before lunch, to bowing farewells at the end of the day. These formal bows are structurally, contextually, and culturally determined.

An example of an informal bodily technique can be seen is the hair-pulling fight in the Madoka video, a fight we have discussed in the earlier chapters on *mimamoru* and *gyarari*. Here, we analyze another dimension of this interaction: Why don't Nobu and Yusuke bow to each other when they apologize at the end of the long discussion of their fight? At the end of this interaction, Kaizuka has her arms around the two boys. Holding them close to her and to each other makes it difficult for them to do a formal bow and

Figure 4.6. Bowing.

Figure 4.7. Tilting the head to the side.

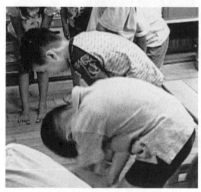

Figure 4.8. Bowing.

Figure 4.9. Tilting the head and body.

Figure 4.10a–c. Madoka teachers' morning meeting.

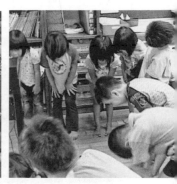

Figure 4.11a–c. Morning opening, lunch, and departure.

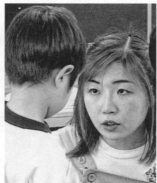
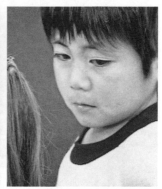

Figure 4.12a–c. Holding two boys too close to bow, eye contact, and tears.

instead encourages eye contact. In this way, Kaizuka has cued the boys that what is called for here is not the formality of a bow, but instead the expression of heartfelt feeling, in the form of tears and eye contact (figure 4.12a–c).

INTERCORPOREAL HYBRIDITY

When Toshi initially apologizes to Maki, he does a quick, short bow. His bow begins like a formal bow, with a downward dip. But because he wants to maintain eye contact to see if his apology will be accepted, Toshi keeps his head and eyes raised, which interrupts the fluidity of the bow, giving it a feeling less of regret than of eagerness to be forgiven (figure 4.13a–c).

Maki does not accept this initial bow and apology and instead exaggerates how much he has hurt her (figure 4.14a and b). Our guess is that what she is looking for here from Toshi is not an apology so much as a display of empathy. Rather than a bow, she perhaps would prefer that Toshi pat her

Figure 4.13a–c. Toshi's initial apology and bow.

Figure 4.14a and b. Maki holds her chest and drapes herself on the table.

on the back or ask her, "Does it hurt?" Toshi, having misread what is called for and desired in this situation, performs a formal bow in a context that calls for something else—a more heartfelt, informal show of empathy between friends. Toru, who has been watching the interaction from across the room, rushes over to help. He pats Maki on the back (figure 4.15a), which is comforting, but isn't what she is looking for, as it comes from him and not from the person who has hurt her. Toru misreads what is called for in this context when he suggests that Maki tell the teacher (figure 4.15b), which she does not do. When Morita reflected on this scene, she told us that Maki did not tell on Toshi because she knew that his hitting her was an accident and therefore that asking for her teacher to intervene was not the appropriate course of action; Morita said that if Maki or Toru had approached her to complain about Toshi's behavior, she would have encouraged them to handle the situation themselves. Toshi, aware that his initial apology has not

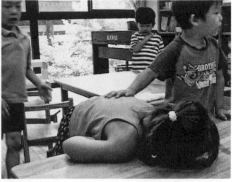

Figure 4.15a and b. Toru comes over, pats Maki's back, and suggests she tell the teacher, as Toshi approaches.

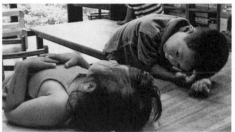

Figure 4.16a and b. Toshi says "Gomen" (sorry) to Maki, as he bends forward.

worked, attempts to mollify Maki by repeatedly saying "Gomen." Eventually he changes tactics and bends down next to her with his torso alongside hers on the table and his head turned toward her (figure 4.16a and b).

We suggest that Toshi's initial bow unsuccessfully combined two embodied forms of apologizing: the formal bow, with no eye contact, and the informal face-to-face, eye-to-eye exchange of feelings (figures 4.17–19). At the end of the hair-pulling fight, we see a successful example of this face-to-face form of apologizing, where with no bowing, few words, and mostly eye contact, the two boys resolve their dispute. Their mutual apologies are successful because they are sincere expressions of regret, performed using bodily techniques of standing very close, with intense eye contact. Toshi's bow is awkward and unsuccessful because the formality of his bend from the waist is undermined by his keeping his head up to maintain eye contact, with the result that he is caught between the two gestures, making his intent unconvincing and his gesture ambiguous. Yamada of Senzan Yōchien pointed out that young children usually maintain eye contact when bowing:

Figure 4.17. Formal bow.   Figure 4.18. Half bow, half eye contact.   Figure 4.19. Eye contact.

TOBIN: Why do you do such a polite bowing with children?

YAMADA: Children need a combination of bowing with eye contact.

TOBIN: Is it difficult for children to do a deep bow without eye contact?

YAMADA: Yes, children usually bow like this [bowing, while keeping eye contact].

Perhaps what eventually makes Toshi's apology work at the end of the interaction is that this time he finds a way to make eye contact while bending in toward Maki, his body twisting away from the vertical plane of the formal bow to the sideways head movement of the informal gesture (figure 4.20).

This sort of corporeal hybridity combining formal and informal registers can be seen as well in other scenes. In the original Preschool in Three Cultures video, Midori, a four-year-old girl, tries to comfort and give advice to her classmate, Satoshi, who has just been hit and stepped on by Hiroki. She does this effectively by bending to the side, as she leans in toward him, allowing her to make eye contact while communicating concern (figure 4.21). At the end of the teddy bear scene, we see a more awkward version of corporeal hybridity when Seiko bows to Nao but keeps her eyes up (figure 4.22), much as Toshi initially did with Maki. What makes Seiko's bow awkward, like Toshi's, is that she stays in the vertical (formal) plane, but adds the kind of eye contact associated with informality. Combining bending to the side with eye contact feels fluid because both are informal. Combining bowing with eye contact feels awkward because one gesture is formal, the other informal.

Figure 4.20. Successful hybrid gesture.

Figure 4.21. Midori's fluent gesture.

Figure 4.22. Seiko's awkward gesture.

BODILY CITATIONALITY

Straightness (*pi*), like the vertical bow, is associated with formality. At Madoka, to mark the beginning of lunch, Kaizuka says to the children, "Osenaka pi" (Straighten your back) (figure 4.23). Children then stand up straight (or at least straighten) and say "Itadakimasu," as they bow (more or less) in unison. At Komatsudani, at the beginning of the formal closing, Morita says, "Ki o tsuke no pi" (Stand at attention) (figure 4.24). Children then straighten their backs and put their arms at their sides in anticipation of the exchange of farewell greetings. During such structured activities that call for stylized bodily techniques we see clear parallels between the bodily techniques of teachers and of their students, who imitate them with varying degrees of fidelity.

Figure 4.23. "Straight backs."

Figure 4.24. "Stand at attention."

Even when their teachers are not present, children often imitate them. The pee lesson at Komatsudani is such an example of a child citing a teacherly corporeal practice and attitude. At Komatsudani, every day after lunch five of the five-year-old children who are that day's *tōban* (daily helpers) put on aprons and go downstairs to help care for the infants and toddlers. As *tōban*, the older children employ different bodily and speech registers than they do when they play with younger children during free play. As Morita explained, "When children are *tōban*, they use a different level of formality." In the pee lesson (figure 4.25a–f), five-year-old Kenichi stands straight next to two-year-old Taro and uses a relatively formal directive speech register, as well as stiff, upright posture, as he issues commands such as, "Oshiiko shinasai" (Please pee). Kenichi then gives a series of direct detailed instructions to Taro on how to pee, reminding him to lift up his pajama top, to aim, and to make sure he is done peeing before pulling up his pajama bottoms. Kenichi ends his hands-on lesson with a warning that he is about to flush the urinal. As he does so, his posture and demeanor change, as he performs a look of mock fear and surprise, mimicking and parodying a version of a toddler's response to the noise of the flush, and then waving off this concern with a gesture of "just kidding." At this point Kenichi looks right at the camera (or camera man) and smiles, in an informal gesture we interpret as a statement of one mature person to another: "Wasn't that cute!" With this last gesture Kenichi's demeanor shifts from the formal teacherly register he used during the pee lesson to an informal demeanor that communicates the kind of collective joy in the body Bakhtin categorized under the heading of the carnivalesque.

Figure 4.25a. "Pee, please."

Figure 4.25b. Standing straight.

Figure 4.25c. "Aim your pee-pee this way."

Figure 4.25d. "Now I am going to flush."

Figure 4.25e. Mock surprise.

Figure 4.25 f. Looking at the camera.

During the *tōban* period we see other scenes of older children imitating adult ways of caring for babies and toddlers (figure 4.26a–d). We see a five-year-old girl, as she puts a clean shirt on a toddler, watching her teacher doing the same thing with a baby. We see a five-year-old boy feeding a baby, sticking a spoon too far into the baby's mouth, while a teacher looks on, giving encouragement to both of them. We also see an older boy matching a teacher's gesture of holding arms out to encourage a baby to take his first steps unassisted. Then, when the baby gives up walking and switches to crawling, two older boys drop down to the floor and crawl alongside him, in a corporeal expression that mixes empathy with parody.

We see another example of bodily citationality at the beginning of the lunch ceremony at Madoka. Each day, several *tōban* stand in front of their classmates and lead the pre-meal greeting of "Itadakimasu" following the lead of their classroom teacher, Kaizuka. Figure 4.27a and b shows the synchronization of the bodily movements of Kaizuka and one of the day's four *tōban*, Sakura. Their bows start with straight backs and hands clasped. As the greeting comes to an end, Sakura breaks her vertical positioning by turning to look at Kaizuka to see when it is okay to stand back up.

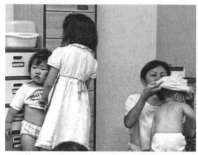

Figure 4.26a. Helping change clothes.

Figure 4.26b. Feeding a baby.

Figure 4.26c. Encouraging a baby to walk.

Figure 4.26d. Crawling alongside the baby.

Figure 4.27a and b. Sakura (on right) imitates Kaizuka's hand position and posture.

We see another example of children citing adult bodily movements during the morning opening at Meisei School for the Deaf. We see Norie turn to the girl next to her, Erika, to instruct her to keep her legs together. We

Figure 4.28a and b. "It's better to close your legs."

Figure 4.28c. Norie points to Erika's legs.　　Figure 4.28d. Erika follows Norie's instruction.

interpret her concern here as not so much for gender modesty, as for not intruding on another's space and of the need to sit more formally during a more formal context of the school day. Norie first signs to Erika: "It's better to close your legs." Norie then demonstrates this posture with her legs and points to Erika's legs, at which point Erika follows Norie's instructions and closes her legs (figure 4.28a–d). Norie's bodily demeanor during this interaction is teacherly, reminiscent of the way girls when they play school with their dolls perform exaggerated versions of pedagogical authority.

THE SPATIALITY OF EMBODIMENT

In all three Japanese preschools where we made videos, we see children moving freely from classrooms to hallways to playgrounds, as they engage in

Figure 4.29a. Lining up.

Figure 4.29b. Navigating hall traffic.

Figure 4.29c. Sitting and standing close.

Figure 4.29d. Co-sleeping.

both structured and nonstructured activities. Preschools are complex physical environments where children engage in a range of complex social interactions. In these spaces each child learns not only bodily techniques for controlling his or her own body, but also intercorporeal techniques for interacting with classmates in socially structured ways, practicing what Erving Goffman (1971) calls "the spatiality of embodiment."

We see such an intercorporeal flow of children across spaces and contexts in the videos that show children lining up; passing each other as they flow by on staircases and in the hallways; sitting together; and sleeping together (figure 4.29a–d). These are among the embodied routines that make up life in preschool, routines that mirror life in the larger society. They are more tightly bunched than seems necessary, perhaps to allow them to hear their teacher clearly on the noisy playground, but no one pushes or complains. They walk inside in a bunch, without colliding, perhaps enjoying the corporeal and social closeness.

As Erving Goffman explains, the intercorporeal synchronization of bodies in space is a basic feature of social behavior. Young children have opportunities in preschool to learn to negotiate space and position across changing

Figure 4.30. Establishing spacing.

contexts. They quickly become adept at how to walk in a line and pass each other in hallways without bumping and how close to be to others when they sit and sleep. As Director Kumagai of Senzan Yōchien explained:

KUMAGAI: The three-year-old children enter preschool in April and it doesn't take longer than the end of May for them to learn how to put away their shoes and bags when they arrive each day, to line up to greet each other, to participate in morning exercises, and to move inside as a group for the start of the morning opening.

HAYASHI: Do the teachers have to teach this to children?

KUMAGAI: No, this isn't something children need to be taught directly. They pick it up on their own.

TOBIN: What happens if a child doesn't follow what the group is doing?

KUMAGAI: We wouldn't pressure him. He will eventually come around. Actually, I'm surprised each spring at how quickly the three-year-olds master these routines.

We see another example of such intercorporeality at Madoka where, after changing into their swimsuits, children line up to go outside for their swimming lesson. They spontaneously touch the shoulders or back of the child in front of them to establish distance and coordinate their movement (figure 4.30), allowing for a synchronization of many bodies into a collective activity.

We also see children using a variety of techniques to facilitate the flow of bodies in shared spaces. Goffman points out that in such social contexts as

Figure 4.31. Helping hands.   Figure 4.32. Helping hands.

walking on a crowded sidewalk the usually smooth flow of bodies occasionally breaks down when people jostle each other or pull up face to face, in an
awkward standoff about who has the right of way. The flow of bodies in space
requires techniques of recovery, strategies for how to get back in the flow
with the minimum of effort, negotiation, or apology. In preschools, teachers
occasionally intervene when they sense flow is about to break down. More
often teachers hold back and don't intervene in order to allow students to
experience discomfort and have the opportunity to restore order on their
own. Bumping into a classmate, like fighting, does not constitute a social
breakdown—Japanese teachers see these as forms of social interaction.
Bumping, jostling, touching, and even hitting are forms of intercorporeal
dialogue.

In figure 4.31, we see Kenichi preparing for his helper job by donning an
apron. When he has trouble, another boy helps him tie his apron strings. In
figure 4.32, a boy is holding a large beetle and another boy holds his hand,
as if to provide both physical and emotional support. In both interactions
children wordlessly offer and accept support, allowing the flow of classroom
life to proceed.

Much of the touching in Japanese preschools is implicit and subtle, less
definite than a hug or kiss, taking the form of spontaneously patting a back,
touching an arm, brushing a shoulder, leaning against someone in line, or
stroking someone's hair (figure 4.33a–d).

In this chapter we have explored how Japanese children learn techniques
of the body. We have suggested that a fundamental goal of Japanese preschools is to function as a place where young children learn characteristically Japanese corporeal practices. This means not just or primarily master-
ing a set of rules, but also learning to read what is called for in a context and

Figure 4.33a and b. Pats on the back.

Figure 4.33c and d. Touching a friend's or teacher's hair.

doing it with bodies as well as words. The pedagogical strategy teachers most often use to support this learning emphasizes the role of embodied experience over didactic instruction or abstract, decontextualized discussion, what Scott Clark (1998) in his paper on how children learn the etiquette of the public bath, calls "embedded tutoring" (240). The goal is for children gradually to conform to the contextual norms of the Japanese classroom not because of pressure or a feeling of obligation, but out of a desire to participate in social interaction.

Chapter 5

—

Expertise

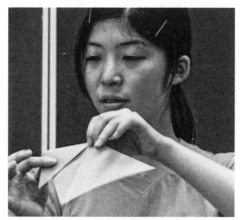

Figure 5.1.

THE ORIGAMI ACTIVITY

In the Komatsudani video we see Morita holding up a stack of brightly colored origami paper as she says, "I wonder, what color fish should I make? Who wants to use blue? Raise your hands. Okay, now who wants yellow? Here you go. Hold on, I'll bring it over to you." Once each of the children has a sheet of square paper, Morita folds her paper in half, saying, "First we make a triangle. That's right. Our fish are now triangles. And then fold in both sides, right, like that, just like when you make a tulip. Then fold the two corners in, like this. And one more fold, like this. Got it? Good. No? Here, I'll help you."

Once the children have folded their papers into the shape of fish, Morita says, "It seems so sad without a mouth or eyes. What should we do? I'll take a marker, and draw an eye on my fish, like this." When the children finish folding and drawing their fish they bring them over to Morita, who writes their names on the back and attaches a metal clip, which the children will use later to catch the fish with magnets on the end of bamboo poles. Morita next announces that it is time for swimming.

When we interviewed Morita shortly after shooting the video, she had little to say about the origami activity. At the time, she was twenty-five years old, in her third year of teaching. When we returned to Komatsudani Hoikuen ten years later, in 2012, to interview her about how she had changed as a teacher over the years, Morita was in her thirteenth year of teaching. When we sat down with Morita, her former co-teacher and now the school's head teacher Takaya Nogami, and Director Yoshizawa, all three commented on this scene, all pointing out her tendency, as a young teacher, of always seeming to be in a rush:

> TOBIN: What are your reactions to watching the video?
> MORITA: It seems like I was in a hurry all the time. It's like I felt I had to explain the origami activity. I talked and talked, and kept up this kind of one-way talking, right through the origami activity, and then into lunch, talking and talking like this, from one activity to the next, throughout the day.
> NOGAMI: Yeah, right. It seems like you continually were focused on what *you* had to do next. Therefore we can say that you hadn't yet reached the point as a teacher that you could really *see* each child.

Mariko Kaizuka was in her fourth year of teaching in 2002 when we shot the video in her classroom at Madoka Yōchien. When we visited Madoka in 2012 to interview her again, Kaizuka was not teaching, having taken a leave in 2006, after eight years of teaching, to start a family. Her twin sons, born in 2007, were students at Madoka from 2010 to 2012, which kept her in contact with the school and gave her the opportunity to see the school from a parental as well as teacher's perspective. (She returned to teaching at Madoka in 2014, two years after we interviewed her.)

We watched the Madoka video with Kaizuka and her former and current directors, Yoshio Machiyama and his son Taro. When we reached the point where Kaizuka mediates the hair-pulling fight between two boys, she stopped the video and commented, "Yoyū ga nai." Morita used this same phrase to describe how she taught early in her career. *Yoyū* can be translated into English as room, time, flexibility, or composure. *Yoyū ga nai* then means lacking time, space, or composure or being in a rush. Both teachers suggested that they had a greater sense of composure, of *yoyū*, later in their careers than they had in their early years of teaching.

In chapter 1 we presented comments from teachers who reported how they resist the impulse to intervene in children's disputes and we quoted a preschool director who said: "It takes at least five years for a teacher to learn to do *mimamoru*." This and similar quotes made us wonder what it is about resisting the impulse to intervene that takes so long to master. What is it that gives veteran teachers a sense of time, space, and composure they can see, in retrospect, they lacked as beginners? What is expert preschool teaching in Japan? How is it acquired? In this chapter we use our interviews with Morita and Kaizuka and other Japanese preschool teachers and administrators to identity emic answers to these questions and to explore how these Japanese perspectives both confirm and, in some cases, challenge the literature on the development of teaching expertise.

THE PROBLEM OF STUDYING EXPERTISE

We suggest that asking experienced teachers to watch a video showing them teaching at a beginning stage of their career represents a useful methodological innovation in research on the development of expertise. The transition from novice to expert is not well understood (Berliner 1988). Most studies of teaching expertise have relied on comparisons of novice and expert teachers, based on either observations or questionnaires administered to beginning and experienced teachers. For example, Paul Schempp and his colleagues (1998) interviewed novice and more experienced teachers. They found the more experienced teachers were better at interpreting classroom events and adjusting their pedagogy to their students, and they took more responsibility for their students' learning. Another approach is the quasi-experimental studies conducted by David Berliner and his colleagues, who showed beginning and experienced teachers photos of classrooms and then asked them to recall what they had seen. The novice teachers' descriptions tended to be literal: "A room full of students sitting at a table," "A blond-haired boy at the table, looking at papers." In contrast, the more experienced teachers saw deeper meanings and pedagogical principles in the pictures: "It's a group of students maybe doing small group discussion on a project as the seats are not in rows" (Berliner 1988, 12).

Studies of these types can reveal provocative differences between novices and experts, but not *how* novices become expert. As Berliner (1988), Feiman-Nemser and Floden (1986), and Zeichner and Gore (1990), among others, have pointed out, because it takes many years to become an expert teacher, and because such expertise is the result of many factors, it is difficult to pinpoint the key processes of teachers' development.

A related area of research is induction into teaching. Studies of induction focus on the transition from university student to beginning teacher and on the contributions to successful beginning teaching of preservice and in-service professional development opportunities (Feiman-Nemser 2001). Our approach to studying the development of teaching expertise differs from induction studies in that we focus not on the first one to three years of teaching, as in most induction studies, but instead on change that occurs after the fifth year. Three years is enough time to be inducted into teaching, but, at least according to our Japanese informants, not long enough to become an expert teacher.

Another related area of research is on lesson study (Lewis 2009) and more generally on structured professional development activities (Ball and Cohen 1999; Paine 1990; Paine and Fang 2007; Sato, Chung Wei, and Darling-Hammond 2008). Studies in this area of research focus less on how teachers change over time than on how educational systems structure professional development opportunities. Our approach is different in that we are interested not only in the impact of such explicit, well-structured professional development activities as lesson study, but also in nonexplicit, unstructured experiences that contribute to the development of expertise, what Scott Clark (1998) calls "embedded tutoring" and John Singleton (1998) calls "implicit cultural pedagogies in social settings" (14).

Most studies of expertise, induction, and professional development have focused on primary and secondary teachers and on the development of skills for teaching mathematics and science. While there are presumably some truths of expert teaching that apply to all levels of education and all content areas, teaching preschool well requires a special set of skills and perspectives. This is related to what Rand Spiro and his colleagues (1992) call the problem of studying professional practice in "ill-structured domains." The tasks to be accomplished in a high school algebra class are much clearer than in a preschool classroom. Furthermore, as our previous research suggests, there are reasons to believe that Japanese preschool classrooms, compared with their counterparts in the United States, China, and many other coun-tries, are especially ill structured, in the sense of having less specific learning outcomes and, as we discuss in chapter 6, fewer curriculum guidelines. We suggest that the less well structured the domain to be mastered, the more difficult the task of identifying differences between beginners and experts and the processes by which expertise is acquired.

This chapter introduces a Japanese perspective that can challenge and deepen understandings both of teaching expertise and of mechanisms for the development of expertise. As anthropologists, we view becoming an ex-pert teacher as a process of enculturation, not just of socialization or profes-sionalization (Zeichner and Gore 1989).

CONCEPTUALIZING DIFFERENCES BETWEEN NOVICES AND EXPERTS

Time, Space, and Composure

Both Morita's and Kaizuka's first reaction after watching a video of them-selves teaching ten years earlier was "Yoyū ga nai." This phrase can refer either to a lack of adequate time or space to maneuver, or to a lack of *aware-ness* of the time and space that could have been used, as in such statements as "I rushed too much because I didn't realize that I had more time than I thought I had." In other words, *yoyū ga nai* is a phrase that can refer either to objective temporal and spatial constraints on action, or to the subjective experience of feeling hurried or fenced in. For situations in which there were objective pressures demanding quick action, *yoyū ga nai* can be trans-lated into English as "I had to hurry." For situations in which people act more quickly and frantically than they needed to, a more apt translation would be "I rushed it." It is this second meaning of the phrase, the sense of retrospec-tively realizing that one acted with more haste and less composure than one should have, that we take as Morita's and Kaizuka's meaning and that we sug-gest is a central metaphor for the difference between early-career and more experienced teachers.

In our discussion at Komatsudani, Morita, Nogami, and Director Yoshi-zawa commented on dimensions of *yoyū* as they reflected on the video of Morita teaching ten years earlier:

MORITA: I talked too much. Too full of words. I didn't allow room/
space/time [*yoyū*] for the children's reactions. I was too preoccupied with my own thoughts [*jibun de ippai*].

NOGAMI: You have changed. You now are able to explain things by
showing, not by talking. And when you do talk, you talk to each
child, and not to the whole class.

YOSHIZAWA: It seems like ten years ago you tried to do everything in the proper way. It's like you were following all the rules,
like according to the way you were taught at the university. With
experience, and especially having experiences of failure, you have
gradually changed.

The staff at Komatsudani told us that over the last ten years little has
changed in the school's daily routines, facilities, enrollment, regulations,
or student/teacher ratios. And as Nogami commented after watching the
video: "It's good to see that the children haven't changed." This suggests that
Morita's sense of being less hurried now than she was ten years ago reflects
not a change of conditions or the tasks of teaching, but instead a change in
her subjective experience of time and space and maturation in her awareness of the possibilities of action within the constraints she works under.
The comments by Morita, Nogami, and Yoshizawa emphasize how Morita
changed from always feeling rushed to feeling composed; from talking to
showing; and from one-sided to reciprocal conversations. In describing
their teaching ten years ago with the phrase *yoyū ga nai*, these teachers are
saying not "I didn't have enough time" but rather "I acted *as if* I didn't have
time (when in reality I did)."

The ability to retain composure under pressure, to take time to slow
down, allowing for nuanced decision-making under tense conditions that
demand action (or holding back), has been attributed to skilled, experienced
soldiers and policemen, (Grossman 2009; Klinger 2006), pilots (Hutchins
and Klausen 1996), surgeons (Polanyi 1966; Hindmarsh and Pilnick 2007),
and athletes (Jackson 1996). We are not suggesting that the stakes of making
a mistake are as high in a preschool classroom as on the battlefield, in an
operating room, in a cockpit, or on a World Cup soccer field. What we are
suggesting is that to perform at a high level in each of these settings requires
a similar ability to slow things down in order to make good, on-the-spot decisions, an ability that takes years to master.

Emptiness

Morita described her earlier teaching as "jibun de ippai." This is tricky to translate. *Jibun* means "oneself." *Ippai* means "full of." Together, these words can be translated as "preoccupied by my own thoughts" or "too much in my head." We take the meaning of Morita's comment here to mean, as Director Yoshizawa explained, that the inexperienced version of Morita was too focused on following the rules and procedures she had in her head from her days as a university student and her preconceived plans and expectations, and that this preoccupation worked to prevent her from focusing instead on the children in front of her.

A consequence of being too focused on the daily schedule, too concerned with acting properly, and too much in one's head is a loss of spontaneity and an inability to respond to the unexpected and to be responsive to children. Berliner (1988) suggests that a difference between beginning and experienced teachers is that experienced teachers are able to adjust their lessons as they interact with children. This is consistent with Morita's comment that ten years earlier in her career she had trouble letting go of her determination to march the children through planned lessons and the daily schedule and with Director Yoshizawa's observation that Morita over the years has become gradually more flexible and able to adjust to the situation in front of her.

In the interviews at both Komatsudani and Madoka our informants used the metaphor of scripts and instructions. As Director Yoshizawa of Komatsudani explained:

> There are things that we have rules for and things where we don't have any rules. In a childcare center, there are rules about safety. But we don't have any rules about children. There is no manual. Therefore, it's up to us what we do.

And Director Taro Machiyama of Madoka commented:

> It's not like we have a manual. It's not like we hand a new teacher a manual and say: "Here, you should memorize these things in your first year." I think this situation is common in the field of Japanese early childhood education. I'm not saying this is good or bad. I'm just saying that this situation is common.

The absence of manuals, lesson plans, and teaching scripts requires Japanese preschool teachers to be able to tolerate ambiguity and respond creatively and nonrigidly to situations that arise in their classroom. In our interviews many Japanese early childhood educators used the term *sunao* to describe the character of an expert preschool teacher. *Sunao* often is translated into English as "obedient." However, the Japanese early childhood educators in our interviews used *sunao* more in the sense of the English expressions "open-minded," "open-hearted," "cooperative," and "sincere." White and LeVine (1986) identify *sunao* as one of the key terms Japanese mothers list in their definition of an *iiko* (a good child) and that teachers value in students. We suggest that *sunao* is also a key characteristic of a good teacher. For example, a preschool director in Tokyo faulted Kaizuka for a lack of *sunao* in her approach to the children's accusations of hair pulling and pinching in the 2002 video:

> If she didn't see the beginning of the fight, why didn't she just listen to the children's explanation and accept it? If she did see it, why didn't she tell the children that she saw it? To be a good teacher it is important to be *sunao*.

For a teacher to be *sunao* means listening to what children say without judgment, preconception, or a predetermined response, and reciprocating children's open-minded, open-hearted sincerity.

Hiroshi Azuma (1994) describes this stance as "empty mindedness." Azuma suggests that true understanding is impossible if one does not make his or her mind clean and empty when listening to others. This is consistent with Spiro, Collins, and Ramchandran's (2007) argument that ill-structured domains (such as preschool teaching) require expert practitioners to employ

> complex, open, and flexible habits of mind. . . . .that foster the building of knowledge characterized by multiple representation, interconnectedness, contingency, and context-dependence, a tendency to recognize when it is appropriate to say 'it depends' and to acknowledge that many situations are not 'either/or,' but rather shades of gray in between. (20).

We see parallels between the concept of empty-mindedness, the psychoanalyst's skill of attentive listening, anthropology's attitude of nonjudgmental cultural relativism, and Zen aesthetics and ethics. Zen emphasizes the notion of *satoru* (empty your mind) as a key to becoming a mature person. An empty mind is different from ignorance. A related Zen term, *mushin*, means making your mind empty. Psychoanalysts, anthropologists, and Zen masters all have terms to describe the skills of receptivity and tolerating ambiguity.

Our informants suggest these skills are also found in the expert preschool teacher, who should be flexible, tolerate ambiguity, not have fixed ideas, accept ideas from children, pay attention to children, and adjust her behavior to the particular child and the ever-changing context. As Kaizuka suggests, over time a teacher needs to learn to be less in her head and more present, which requires one to be empty—of fixed notions, preconceptions, and scripts.

Attention

Both Morita and Kaizuka told us, and their directors concurred, that when they were newer to teaching they had difficulty knowing where to place their attention and balancing the needs of the class as a whole with those of individual children, as we can see in this reflection by Kaizuka on her mediation in the argument between the two boys while the rest of the class was changing clothes:

> Kaizuka: I didn't use space and time well here [*Yoyū ga nakatta no kana*]. I wish I had been able to pay more attention to the other children when I was dealing with those two boys.
> Machiyama: I totally understand what you mean. By your ninth year of teaching you would pay attention to the other children. That's the difference. This was only your fourth year of teaching.

Kaizuka sees a weakness of her early teaching as a tendency to focus her attention too narrowly on one or two children at a time, while ignoring the rest of the class. On the other hand, inexperienced teachers can also err in the opposite direction, by focusing too much attention on the class as a whole and too little on individual children, as Morita felt she did during the origami lesson and other times in the day when she marched the group through activities. Expert teaching, therefore, is defined as a balance between attending to the needs of individual students and the group.

Knowing and Trusting Children

In our interviews at both Komatsudani and Madoka, the teachers and directors suggested that with experience, teachers learn to know and trust children, which allows them to individualize the way they interact with the children and to predict situations in their classroom:

> HAYASHI: Did the way you deal with children change between your fourth year and ninth year of teaching?
>
> KAIZUKA: I changed over the years. At the beginning of my teaching career I thought I had to behave the same way with everyone, for example, to scold everyone the same way and get their attention the same way. But with experience, I gradually changed and learned to scold and get attention in different ways with different children.
>
> TOBIN: Would you say that such change with time is typical in teachers?
>
> MACHIYAMA: It should be that way. Teachers should change how they deal with children depending on each child. But not everyone does.

Nogami made a similar point:

> HAYASHI: What is the difference between new teachers and experienced teachers?
>
> NOGAMI: The ability to *see* children. Not only to see them, but also to be able to judge what kind of children they are, and the ability to predict what this child might do in various situations.

Director Yoshizawa said that he emphasizes to new teachers the importance of learning to know the character of each child in their class as soon as possible after the school year begins in April:

> Around June each year, Nogami-sensei comes to tell me, "We are getting to know the children." What he means is we now know each child's personality and habits, how each child might act in certain situations, and how the children in the class interact. Therefore we tell teachers including new teachers to observe children as much as possible.

Nogami suggested that in addition to knowing children, new teachers also need to learn to trust them:

> NOGAMI: New teachers intervene quickly in children's fights because they are afraid that children might do something wrong or terrible. Or new teachers try to keep their children inside the classroom because they get nervous if their children are out of their sight. Or for example, they stop children from playing in the mud. I won't stop children from doing that. I would just think, "It's no big deal; we can wash them off."
>
> TOBIN: Do you say this to new teachers?
>
> NOGAMI: Yes, I tell them, "Please don't act so strongly. Children won't do terrible things. They know what they can do and can't do."

Understanding Children's Amae

In chapter 2 we introduced the concept of *amae*, which Takeo Doi argued is a basic human need that is given great salience in Japanese culture. *Amae,* according to Doi, is an expression of the desire to be cared for by others. In a follow-up interview with Morita and Nogami of Komatsudani, they emphasized that with experience they had learned to understand children's expression of *amae* and to respond to these expressions with more nuance and better judgment. Morita gave the example of how she has changed over time in something as simple-seeming as deciding whether to help a child with her shoes:

> Of course it's quicker if I help a child put her shoes on, especially when we are short on time. In my second year of teaching I often made that kind of mistake. I helped them too often and too quickly, which means I took away from children the chance to grow up on their own. It was like I thought my job was to put their shoes on, or my job was to take care of children. Student teachers tend to put shoes on children when they look for help. I tell them: "Wait." Then student teachers are like, "Then what am I supposed to do?" It's like then they are just standing around, because they don't have anything to do. Actually it is our job to wait and watch [*mimamoru*], but they haven't got that far yet. The first year of teaching, we think our job is to help.

Nogami added: "It's like early in my career, I defined my job as taking care of children. But as I gained experience, I came to see my central task as attending to children's development."

Nogami connected three of our central concepts—*amae*, *mimamoru*, and *omoiyari*—in his explanation of the difference between himself as a beginning and experienced teacher:

> I think my practice was based on *omoiyari* for myself at the beginning of teaching. In our early years of teaching, it made us feel good about ourselves to think that we were helping children. Or maybe we wanted to get credit from others for helping children. Or we thought the fact that we put their shoes on was evidence of our teaching ability. When children expressed *amae*, we gradually came to be able to do *mimamoru*. This means not using our hands, but our eyes.

Morita suggested that the art of teaching lies in knowing when to help a child and when to hold back, but that this knowing isn't necessarily conscious:

> TOBIN: Is there any tendency to help when you see a child struggling?
>
> MORITA: Well, yeah, I want to help them, but I know they are happy when they discover they can do it on their own. But yes, it is really tough to wait.
>
> HAYASHI: How about when you just started teaching? Your first year of teaching?
>
> MORITA: No, I couldn't. I did everything for them. I didn't wait at all. We have to have *yoyū* [patience] in order to accept children's *amae*, and know when to encourage them to do something on their own and when to give them help and one-to-one attention. It depends on many factors. For example, a child who was born in April [the beginning of the Japanese school year] tends to be able to do many things on her own. Therefore we teachers will spend more time with a child who was born in March. There are days when a child who can do something by herself is feeling a need for me to care for her. I let a child *amaeru* when she is struggling and having a hard time. Accepting children's *amae* is one of the ways to

build relationships with children. *Amae* is like a form of *skinship* (interpersonal closeness through physical connections). But we have to have *yoyū* in order to do this.

HAYASHI: How do you know when to indulge a child's *amae* and when to hold back?

MORITA: It's a feeling, something I sense.

TOBIN: We compare this kind of teaching expertise to the skill of a great soccer player, for whom the game slows down, and he can take his time, seeing where everyone is on the field and what would be the perfect pass to make.

NOGAMI: Cool! I totally agree. For us as teachers there are such moments when we see things slow or stop. Everything slows, and our focus is totally on the children.

Professional Judgment

Michael Polanyi (1962) argues that a key component of expert knowledge is the ability to see beyond the parts to the whole. He begins with the problem of how we recognize faces, arguing that this ability is based not on sorting systematically through each facial feature, but rather on a deeper, tacit awareness of the face as a gestalt, as a whole whose integration is more than the sum of its parts (603). Polanyi applies this argument to the skills of an expert medical diagnostician, who determines what is wrong with a patient and the severity of the condition based not only on separate clinical clues but also on professional intuition (604). Polanyi calls this professional intuition "tacit knowledge," because it is a form of reasoning that is not consciously accessible.

We can extend Polanyi's argument to the ability of a skilled preschool teacher. For example, most Japanese teachers we interviewed were able to identify *mimamoru* as a useful pedagogical strategy. Few were able to identify the embodied practices they employ to "do" *mimamoru*, which leads us to define these embodied practices as forms of tacit professional knowledge. Our interviewees usually were unable to explain why in one situation they intervened and in another they held back. Experienced Japanese preschool teachers' ability to assess a classroom disturbance is based on tacit knowledge similar to that of an experienced physician who can list the factors she looks for when doing a differential diagnosis, but cannot tell you how each factor contributed to her discharging one patient and hospitalizing another who has similar symptoms.

When asked to reflect on her approach to the teddy bear fight, Morita was able to cite several factors that made her more and less concerned: the proximity of the piano made her more concerned; her knowledge that these girls routinely fight in this way made her less concerned. Reflecting on the hair-pulling fight, Kaizuka told us that she sometimes intervenes in such fights and sometimes doesn't, and that this decision depends on many factors. While both teachers were able to list factors they consider in such situations, they struggled to be able to explain how these factors interact to contribute to the professional intuition that leads them to intervene in one situation and not in another. Viewing the videos of themselves teaching ten years earlier, both teachers questioned many of their earlier decisions, suggesting that what had changed with experience was their ability to read children and assess interactions, not by following an algorithm or a checklist, but by reading each situation as a gestalt.

Expertise as Embodied Practice

With experience, teachers' practice becomes more embodied in two related senses of the term. Over time they learn to communicate with children using their words less and their bodies more; and they can act and react without needing either to follow a script or to stop to think, allowing their teaching to be more fluid, spontaneous, and responsive to variations in children and contexts.

In the interviews at both Madoka and Komatsudani, our informants emphasized the value of embodied action over talk. Morita described her teaching nine years ago as "too full of words," and Nogami added, "You now are able to explain things by showing rather than talking." Taro Machiyama, who had recently taken over from his father as Madoka's director, suggested that this is a key difference between new teachers and experienced teachers:

> First-year teachers have a tendency to say things, to tell the children something, like "That's bad!" Tenth-year teachers are like, uh, they keep quiet, create a sort of silent situation in the classroom, that they handle not with words, but with their body. This works to give children the sense of something like, "Is this bad?" or "I am sorry." Tenth-year teachers create an atmosphere and it becomes more of a dialogue and

Figure 5.2a. "That's not clear."   Figure 5.2b. "I'm thinking."   Figure 5.2c. "Now I get it."

Figure 5.2d–f. "They create an atmosphere . . . with their bodies . . . and facial expressions."

more reciprocal. It's not only the teacher telling things to children, but also listening to children.

Perhaps aware of the irony of trying to explain with words the value of teaching with one's body, Taro Machiyama grew animated and used gestures and facial expressions to illustrate and emphasize his point (figure 5.2a–f):

HAYASHI: You mentioned that teachers create an atmosphere with their body. Could you explain more about how they do this?
MACHIYAMa: With everything, like facial expressions, including sadness, loneliness, anger, and happiness, or thoughtfulness. They try to show what's in their mind, like: "That's not clear," or "Just a second, I'm thinking," or "What do you think?" or "Now I get it." They don't announce a conclusion.

Taro Machiyama's thinking here about the expert teacher's gradual movement away from words is consistent with Maurice Bloch's (1991) suggestion that in complex domains much expert performance is necessarily nonlinguistic:

> A general feature of the kind of knowledge that underlies the performance of complex practical tasks . . . requires that it be non-linguistic. . . . Probably some teaching needs to be done verbally, but there are also advantages in the non-linguistic transmission of practical skills . . . [that] by-passes the double transformation from implicit to linguistically explicit knowledge made by the teacher and from linguistically explicit to implicit knowledge made by the learner. (187)

Bloch suggests that the ability of an expert practitioner to act in certain domains must be nonlinguistic because the translation of ideas and actions into and out of words would reduce the fluidity these domains and contexts demand. Polanyi (1962) writes of such activities as swimming and piano playing: "If we succeeded in focusing our attention completely on the elements of a skill, its performance would be paralyzed altogether" (601). Berliner (1988) makes a parallel point in his summary of the stages of the development of expertise in teachers:

> If novices, advanced beginners, and competent performers are rational, and proficient performers are intuitive, we might categorize experts as "arational." They have an intuitive grasp of a situation and seem to sense in nonanalytic, nondeliberative ways the appropriate response to make. They show fluid performance, as we all do when we no longer have to choose our words when speaking or think about where to place our feet when walking. (5)

When we asked Kaizuka at this point in her career how much of her teaching is conscious she replied: "To be honest, once I start a day in the classroom, I am not always conscious."

We suggest that a key difference between beginning and expert teachers is that the experts have become more coordinated and fluid in the use of their bodies as their primary tool of teaching. But when we asked Kaizuka and Morita if they agreed with this hypothesis, and if they would say that over the years they have learned to use their bodies more effectively in the classroom, they were unsure how to respond. Morita told us:

I now feel more comfortable in the classroom. But I don't know about being more skilled with my body. I suppose it must be true that I have become better at this, but I have no consciousness of it. It would be interesting to see a video of myself teaching now to compare with then.

HOW TEACHERS DEVELOP EXPERTISE

Experience (Maybe)

How did these teachers explain their change from *yoyū ga nai* to *yoyū ga aru* (from lacking to having *yoyū*), from being rushed, rigid, and didactic to being composed, spontaneous, and interactive? What helped them learn to teach expertly? These teachers, their directors, and other Japanese early childhood educators we interviewed all gave the same initial answer: *keiken* (experience). The problem with this answer is that it explains less than it seems and leads to circular reasoning. It is like saying that the difference between inexperienced and experienced teachers is that the experienced teachers have more experience teaching. "Experience" is like a black box, a purported mechanism of change that we cannot see into.

Even as our informants told us that experience was crucial for learning to teach well, they conveyed doubt in various ways that this explanation was adequate:

TOBIN: You say that new teachers intervene too quickly in fights.
YOSHIZAWA: It's not like we don't ever intervene in children's fights. There is a point where we should stop them, for example, if children grab something that could be dangerous. But if children don't go too far, then we don't stop them.
HAYASHI: How do teachers get to the point of being able to make that distinction?
MORITA: Experience, maybe?
YOSHIZAWA: Maybe only experience?
NOGAMI: By experience, maybe?

In conversation Japanese interlocutors often add *kana* (maybe) to the end of a sentence to soften their statement and to seek the listener's confirmation of the reasonableness of what they are saying. In this case we see something additional going on. We believe that by adding "maybe" to the end of their answers, these informants are suggesting doubt, not doubt that experience is necessary for the development of expertise, but doubt that experience alone can be an adequate explanation.

Even with experience, some teachers do not become expert because something else is lacking, as Taro Machiyama explained to us:

> TOBIN: Do most of the teachers you hire become good teachers?
>
> MACHIYAMA: That's the challenge for us. Teachers need *sense*. If they don't have sense, they can understand what more experienced teachers tell them, but they can't turn this advice into practice. They get the same advice over and over, but they can't benefit from it.

Machiyama's explanation left us wondering: What is this "sense" that expert teachers have and inexpert teachers lack?

Unsatisfied with "experience" and "sense" as answers to our question about the source of teachers' expertise, we asked our informants follow-up questions about a number of the influences on professional growth cited in the literature, influences including lesson study and other explicit professional development activities; apprenticeship learning; feedback from superiors and fellow teachers; and trial-and-error learning. Their answers suggest that becoming an expert teacher requires a combination of a little or a lot of each of these ingredients and, we will suggest, something more.

Explicit Professional Development Activities

Lesson study (*jugyō kenkyū*) is often cited as the key ingredient of Japanese professional development (Lewis 2009; Lewis, Perry, and Murata 2006) and as a main contributor to Japan's success on international achievement tests (Stigler and Hiebert 1999). As Shelley Friedkin (1999) writes:

> In Japan, teachers improve their teaching through "lesson study," a process in which teachers jointly plan, observe, analyze, and refine actual classroom lessons called "research lessons." Lesson study is widely credited for the steady improvement of Japanese elementary mathematics and science instruction.

However, our informants rarely credited lesson study and other formal professional development activities as playing an important role in their development as preschool teachers. For example, when we asked our informants at Komatsudani about lesson study, Nogami replied: "We don't have *these things* at our daycare center." We hear in his use of the phrase "these things" the suggestion not just that they don't do lesson study at his school, but that the kind of systematic development and critique of discrete lessons that primary and secondary teachers use for improving their mathematics instruction couldn't have any useful role at Komatsudani. Taro Machiyama told us that at Madoka the teachers engage in *ennai kenshū* (within-school teacher study sessions) several times a year on topics nominated by teachers, but that he thinks such sessions play a very small part in teachers' development.

HAYASHI: What changes teachers?
MACHIYAMA: First of all, this may not be essential, but I should mention *ennai kenshū*.
TOBIN: Is that an important cause of change?
MACHIYAMA: No, it's not the main reason. The essential part is [looking over to Kaizuka to speak] . . .
KAIZUKA: Probably, to be honest with you, it just doesn't work if we use the same way with everyone. If we do the same way with this child, and with that child, the same way won't work to reach everybody's heart. One child may get this, but not the other one. So we ask ourselves, what can I do? Which approach should I use with this child? It takes time to figure out.

Machiyama and Kaizuka seem to be implying here that lesson study and other systematic professional development activities cannot play an essential role in the development of preschool teaching expertise because young children are so diverse in their characters and needs and early childhood educational contexts so varied and nuanced that there is no single or best way of approaching a lesson or a problem.

An explanation for our informants' reluctance to cite lesson study as an important contributor to their professional development would be that in Japanese preschools, *yōchien* as well as *hoikuen*, lessons make up a very small part of the schoolday and are seen as less important than children's free play and spontaneous interactions. The central goal is children's social-emotional development, which is believed to be a natural process that, like language acquisition, requires teachers to cultivate qualities such as empathy, patience, and restraint rather than to acquire technical knowledge or skills that can be taught and learned systematically.

Most but not all of our informants told us that systematic professional development activities are neither common nor necessary for preschool teachers. One exception was the professors of early childhood education we interviewed, who conduct professional development activities for preschool teachers and directors. It is not surprising that early childhood experts who do in-service professional development as part of their jobs would see such training as efficacious or even as necessary to becoming an expert teacher. Workshops offered by professors and other experts are especially common in university-attached (e.g., laboratory) preschools, and much less common in private *yōchien* and in *hoikuen*, which are the largest sectors of early childhood education and care in Japan.

Apprenticeship Learning

Apprenticeship has been studied as a Japanese pedagogy for acquiring expertise in the arts (Singleton 1998; DeCoker 1998), but not often in education, where formal apprenticeships are rare. Only one of our informants, Kazuya Sawamura at the Meisei School for the Deaf, reported having learned to teach well from a single mentor. Meisei is a private school, the only school for the deaf in Japan that uses Japanese Sign Language as the primary language of instruction and communication. Because Japan offers no teacher preparation programs in sign language education, the primary mechanism of professional development at Meisei is for a less experienced teacher to apprentice for a year or more in a classroom with a more experienced teacher, as Sawamura did with Ikeda in the Meisei preschool program in his first two years. Ikeda was one of the members of the group that founded Meisei School for the Deaf, and she was the first teacher in Meisei's preschool. Sawamura did not describe his relationship to Ikeda using the word apprentice (*minarai* or *deshi*), but simply answered our question of how he learned to teach deaf children by saying, "Ikeda-sensei." Ikeda explained to us in an interview how she viewed her mentoring role:

IKEDA: In the first few years, I was the only one who could teach effectively in JSL in the Meisei preschool program. So gradually

I worked to raise those coming up behind me [*koushin no ikusei*]. Lately, we are letting them gradually take more and more responsibility. This year I am teaching the infant class. During the first semester I sometimes went to the kindergarten classroom to help. But I saw that when I was in the classroom, children would tend to rely on me and not to listen to Sawamura-sensei. Therefore in order to avoid that situation, I stay away from the kindergarten classroom.

TOBIN: So you chose to leave in order for the other teachers to grow?

IKEDA: Yes. My thinking is that I need to raise those behind me. It's not good if people think I am the only good preschool teacher at Meisei. Both parents and children need to see that different teachers can do the job.

In the public deaf schools as well, it is common for younger teachers to be teamed with more experienced ones, something that is seen both as necessary for working in this technical field and as possible because deaf schools have student/teacher ratios that allow for more than one teacher to be assigned to the same group of students.

In hearing preschools, young, inexperienced, part-time teachers or "floaters" are sometimes hired to assist experienced teachers, which allows them to gain experience before being assigned their own class, but these arrangements are rarely if ever conceptualized as apprenticeships, and they are more about induction than about the development of true teaching expertise, which is believed to take many years. Preschool teachers told us that they learned a lot from watching and imitating their elders (*senpai*), but they did not report having learned to teach well primarily from a single mentor. Kaizuka said:

I learned a lot from watching *senpai* teachers. I tried teaching in certain ways, but it didn't work. So then I talked with our experienced teachers, and sometimes they gave me advice, such as "How about trying it this way?" And sometimes they dealt with children with me.

Our informants emphasized that while they learned from mentors, this process was not one of direct observational learning followed by imitation. Their descriptions are more in line with the forms of tacit knowledge acquisition Polanyi (1966) conceptualizes as "indwelling," which he defines as a gradual internalization not just or primarily of isolated behaviors, but of the emergent overall quality of expertise the master embodies:

> The watcher tries to correlate these moves [of the master] by seeking to dwell in them from outside. He dwells in these moves by interiorizing them. By such exploratory indwelling the pupil gets the feel of a master's skill and may learn to rival him. (30)

As Morita told us:

> I learned from watching *senpai* [my seniors] things like "I could have waited longer" and some useful expressions to use with children. This was helpful, but we need to figure things out on our own. It's not something that somebody could teach me to do. But I was watching Nogami-sensei all the time when I first had my own class in the room next to his.

Feedback

As the above comments suggest, most teachers describe having benefited early in their careers less from formal mentoring than from occasional bits of advice offered by more experienced teachers. Experienced teachers and directors told us that they judiciously parcel out bits of advice to the more junior teachers. For example, Nogami sees his role as the head teacher at Komatsudani chiefly as providing quiet, tactful support and encouragement. He told us he does not conduct workshops or have formal meetings with young teachers and rarely gives direct advice:

> HAYASHI: Do you ever tell young teachers that there is a better way to handle a situation?
>
> NOGAMI: I say something only when I see teachers not focusing on children, like if I happen to see them doing something in order to show off to parents or to other teachers. The only thing I do when new teachers first come to our preschool is to give them advice about children, about children's feelings. I try to tell them about children. That's it. It's important to make distinctions between

what children need to learn and don't need to learn at a certain age. We shouldn't put adult thinking on them.

Director Kumagai of Senzan Yōchien gave a similar answer to our question about when she would give advice to a young teacher:

If I happen to see her doing something that I question, then I would say, "Isn't there perhaps another way to see this situation?'" or "Wow, that was a tough situation, wasn't it?" But I wouldn't directly criticize what she is doing.

Kumagai, like Nogami, used the phrase "If I happen to see . . . ," which suggests that they want to be clear that they see their role not as one of surveillance, but rather as one of making gentle suggestions at opportune moments. These and other experienced educators we interviewed emphasized the need to give critical feedback as gently as possible, in a manner that respects the young teacher's effort and ability to arrive at her own solution. Kaizuka gave us the ultimate example of the minimalist approach experienced teachers can take when observing a young teacher dealing in a less than ideal way with children. She said her comment in such a situation would be, simply, "Chotto," which can be translated into English as "It's a bit . . ." We see a parallel here, which is surely not coincidental, between this low-intervention approach experienced teachers and directors use to support young teachers' professional development and the low-intervention approach Japanese preschool teachers use to support their students' social-emotional development. In both cases the underlying emic pedagogy is one of *mimamoru*—supporting development through watching and waiting, with a minimum of intervention.

Trial-and-Error Learning

Most of our informants reported that young teachers learn to teach well mostly not from workshops, apprenticeships, or direct feedback, but by trial and error. As Machiyama Taro told us:

It's difficult to explain how teachers acquire expertise because these are things that are not taught. It's not like senior teachers tell new ones what to do. This is something that you have to work out on your own: "I tried something. It didn't work. What shall I do next?" This is the process. Teachers are reared on failure.

Similarly, Director Yoshizawa said of Morita's development as a teacher, "With experience, especially having experiences of failure, she gradually changed." Morita responded: "Well, I made a lot of mistakes and had a lot of failures. Then gradually, I learned that this is a one-year-old and this is a four-year old, therefore, we need to change the way we explain things to them."

Morita also emphasized the importance of learning by trial and error, although the metaphor she picked was an odd one:

New teachers lack experience, so they haven't yet developed that kind of sense experienced teachers have. As we get more experience, the sense emerges in us. It's like picking mushrooms: "Oh, we can eat this mushroom, but this one is poisonous." People come to know which mushroom is okay to eat through experience.

We did not point out that expert mushroom hunters must have learned to avoid the deadliest of mushrooms by a process other than trial and error.

Kaizuka offered a more apt metaphor than mushroom hunting, as she compared the process of becoming an expert teacher to becoming a skilled chef: "After dealing with a lot of children, and with more experience, I gradually developed a set of cooking techniques, of ways of teaching, of reacting to kids." Kaizuka's notion of developing a larger repertoire of teaching strategies is consistent with Bloch's and Spiro's notion that experts are those who have mastered a set of techniques and schema that can be put into play in novel situations. Experienced teachers draw on their past experiences both to read contexts and children more quickly and accurately and to respond to each child and each situation with a wider repertoire of tactics. Kaizuka's and Morita's self-reports on their development of expertise as teachers matches well with Bloch's (1991) description of playing chess:

Expert chess players do not differ from novices (who are not complete beginners) in knowing the rules of chess or in performing such motor tasks as moving one piece without knocking the others down. What seems to distinguish the expert from the novice is not so much an ability to handle complex strategic logico-mathematical rules, but rather the possession, in memory, of an amazingly comprehensive and organized store of total or partial chess board configurations, which allows the expert to recognise the situation in an instant so as to know what should be done next. . . . What is surely happening is that the expert is not just remembering many games but that she has developed through long practice a specific apparatus which enables her to remember many games and configurations much more easily and quickly than the non-expert. She has learned how to learn this kind of information. This would explain how the expert can cope, not only with situations which she recognises, but also with situations which are new, so long as they fall within the domain which she has learned to cope with efficiently. (188)

PRESCHOOL TEACHING EXPERTISE AS COLLECTIVE AND CONTEXT SPECIFIC

Perhaps when we asked our informants how a teacher develops expertise, we were asking the wrong question. Our question assumed that expertise is a quality of individual teachers, rather than a collective attribute of a team, and one that is transferable from setting to setting, rather than context-specific. Reviewing our informants' responses, we can see now that many of their comments referred to expertise as a quality of a preschool staff rather than of individuals, and a quality that is specific to the preschool that hired them and where most will spend their entire careers. Taro Machiyama commented: "It's not only children who grow up here. Teachers do as well. The first few years are a time for them to grow up."

Each of the directors we interviewed referred to the idea that their staff is a team and not just a collection of individuals. Members of the team include not just the classroom teachers but also bus drivers, aides, and part-timers. As our informants at Madoka explained:

HAYASHI: How do beginning teachers improve?
YOSHIO MACHIYAMA: First, they must have character [soshitsu].
    That's the most important thing. Second is cooperation [renkei].
    We all nurture the development of children here together. We
    have four free teachers and two assistants who don't have teaching

certificates, but they are helpful because they have been working with us for twenty years.

TARO MACHIYAMA: They don't teach. They are assistants. They are grandmother-like figures at our preschool. Like, they say to children, "That's not good."

KAIZUKA: We are fortunate that we have these kinds of people at our school. It's not only that they help us to set up activities, but also to create a good atmosphere. We all call them "sensei." It's difficult to put into words, but it's like their existence makes our personal relationships smooth.

TARO MACHIYAMA: Their contribution is different from a head teacher who also has twenty years' teaching experience.

These comments suggest that Japanese preschool directors think of expertise as a collective capacity of their staff. It is extraordinarily rare for Japanese preschools to fire teachers or to hire experienced teachers who have worked in other preschools. Instead, they do their initial hiring as wisely as they can, and then do their best to support the staff they have hired to function effectively as members of the team, knowing, as Director Kumagai commented, that some of these teachers will never become experts:

Of course, some teachers never become very good, but then we just need to think about what they can do well and what is their strength, and put them in situations that minimize their weaknesses.

Japanese early childhood educators view expertise as not only collective but also contextual. We often heard phrases in our interviews such as "the spirit of Komatsudani" or "the Madoka way." Nogami emphasized that the continuity reported in *Preschool in Three Cultures Revisited* (2009) between Komatsudani in 1984 and 2004 is the result of socializing new teachers into the Komatsudani philosophy: "Maybe our staff doesn't change that much over the years because our philosophy, which is children-based, stays the same. The only thing I do with new teachers is to talk with them about children. That's our way." Morita agreed: "The way I teach is the Komatsudani way. I might have become a very different kind of teacher if I had been hired by another school."

This model of in-house staff development is typical not just of preschools but also of Japanese companies. Thomas Rohlen (1974), for example, studied how Japanese banks socialize new workers to their particular organizational style and culture. The Japanese paradigm of professional expertise assumes a career spent in one school, as opposed to the model of a teacher acquiring transferable skills she can list on a resume and take with her to her next job.

Private preschools have a continuity of both staff and philosophy, which allows them to have a strong school culture. In *Preschool in Three Cultures Revisited*, Tobin, Hsueh, and Karasawa (2009) write:

> Both Komatsudani and Madoka are private programs where the directors and a few highly experienced teachers play very strong roles in mentoring new staff, establishing a characteristic, even idiosyncratic approach, and maintaining continuity of practice over the course of a generation despite a high staff turnover. (145)

Over the course of their first five years preschool teachers are enculturated into the beliefs, practices, and underlying ethos of their preschool. This enculturation results not from direct instruction or a formal apprenticeship, but from an immersion in a cultural world. The preschool's routines, student/teacher ratios, learning materials, and architecture all play a role in this process of structuring the development of teachers. Van Manen (1995) emphasizes that a skilled teacher's practice, her "pedagogical tact," is attuned to the materiality of her particular school and classroom:

> The practical knowledge of teaching resides in the things that surround us: the physical dimensions of the classroom that I recognize as my room to which my body is adapted. My practical knowledge "is" my felt sense of the classroom, my feeling who I am as a teacher, my felt understanding of my students, my felt grasp of the things that I teach, the mood that belongs to my world at school, the hallways, the staffroom, and of course this classroom. (11)

Even though each teacher has her own classroom and students, we estimate that teachers spend about half of the day in the company of other teachers. The day begins with a long period of free play outside, during which teachers collectively keep an eye on the children. In many preschools, classrooms are separated by sliding walls, which are open about half the time, allowing children as well as teachers from adjoining classes to mingle. Lunch is served in cafeterias in some preschools, and in adjoining classrooms in others. The afternoon generally includes another extended period of free play. This daily structure gives new teachers ample opportunities to watch more experienced ones deal with a range of situations, to discuss issues that arise, and to seek and be offered advice. At Madoka, as part of the daily routine, teachers have a short meeting in the morning in which they talk about children and parents and plan for upcoming events. Teachers told us that they do not have many formal workshops or in-service training activities, but these routine meetings and conversations help develop their understanding of child development and pedagogy.

Teachers as well as directors think about expertise not only or primarily as a characteristic of individual teachers, but rather as a collective characteristic of the staff. Teachers expect directors to assign them to grades and tasks matched to their strengths and weaknesses. Ikeda, the most experienced of the preschool teachers at Meisei and the most skilled at teaching Japanese Sign Language to children, told us that she switches around from year to year, and even during the year, from working with infants, to toddlers, to the older preschoolers, depending on her sense of where she is most needed. She explained to us, "As a fluent JSL speaker, I tend to spend more time with five-year-old children, especially at the end of the school year, because I want them to get ready for the academic study at the elementary school."

This notion of enculturation into the educational approach of a particular school and of collective expertise both expands and challenges the Anglophone literature on professionalism. Some of this literature contrasts the virtues of teachers' becoming more professional, which is defined as being more adept at following the best practices of a field, with the dangers of socialization into the status quo mediocrity of a school. This is a common lament of teacher education faculty, who complain that once students graduate and become public school teachers, they become socialized away from the progressive practices they were taught in the university. John Loughran (2007) writes about science teachers' professional development:

> The challenge, though, is to manage this induction phase in such a way as to encourage the sharing of learning so that the sometimes contradictory messages of socialization do not reinforce the very teaching behaviors that have so shaped many beginning teachers' views of science teaching. (1052)

The Japanese preschools, in contrast, see the influence of university coursework at the preservice and in-service levels as less beneficial in the development of teaching expertise than a teacher's gradual socialization into the culture of her preschool. Japanese preschools define expertise less as a transferrable characteristic than as the ability to contribute to the collective enterprise of the preschool and to embody the ethos of the particular school. That having been said, we would point to an irony that while teachers and directors at Meisei, Madoka, and Komatsudani emphasized the value of teachers' becoming enculturated into their particular approach, from our point of view these approaches looked far more alike than different. By this we mean to suggest not that Japanese teachers are easily interchangeable, but instead that there are aspects of expert Japanese teaching that are widely shared from school to school, one of which, ironically, is the belief that expert teaching is school specific.

Chapter 6

—

Early Childhood Education
Policy as Cultural Practice

Figure 6.1.

As we reached the end of this project we brought together four preschool directors and head teachers for a discussion. At one point we asked: "How do you as a preschool director influence your teachers?" Takaya Nogami of Komatsudani replied: "As little as possible." We hear in this comment an echo of the way the preschool teachers we interviewed explained to us their approach to dealing with children's fights. In this chapter we argue that the logic of minimal intervention operates across levels of Japanese early childhood education, guiding how preschool teachers work with children, how directors work with teachers, and how the Ministry of Education and the Ministry of Health and Welfare work with preschools. In each case, from teacher-child classroom interactions, to personnel supervision, to national curriculum guidelines, we see the presence of *mimamoru*. This is an example of a deep structural pattern running through Japanese culture that can be found in the domains of both policy and practice in Japanese early childhood education.

The focus of this chapter is the relationship between *mimamoru* and other implicit pedagogical practices and policy directives. In the case of early childhood education curriculum and pedagogy, Japanese educational officials follow a hands-off approach. In this chapter we show how this hands-off policy plays out in regular preschool classrooms and then discuss deaf education as the exception, where the government takes a more directive role and issues more explicit guidelines for practice.

MIMAMORU AS POLICY AND PRACTICE

In chapter 1 we suggested that *mimamoru* is a strategy that underlies many Japanese early childhood classroom practices designed to give young children space and time to work problems out on their own. In chapter 5 we suggested that while beginning teachers are familiar with the concept of *mimamoru*, it takes years to develop the expertise needed to effectively apply this pedagogy of restraint. Nogami and other preschool administrators we interviewed emphasized that they give their teachers considerable latitude in their curricular planning and pedagogical practices, mixed with occasional advice. This combination of giving latitude, support, and a minimum of guidance is captured by the single term *mimamoru*.

We might expect such a central pedagogical idea to be articulated in *The Kindergarten Education Guidelines*, or other documents produced by MEXT (the education ministry in charge of *yōchien*) or by Koseirōdōshō (the ministry of social welfare in charge of *hoikuen*). But the MEXT and Koseirōdōshō guidelines say nothing directly about *mimamoru*, or about how this approach can be operationalized as a strategy for staff development or in the classroom.

The Kindergarten Education Guidelines issued by MEXT in 2008 is a thirteen-page document broken into three chapters: "General Provisions," "Aims and Contents," and "Points for Consideration in the Formulation of Instructional Plans." The most specific the document gets is in statements of curricular goals, such as "Experiencing the enjoyment of spending time with teachers and friends," "Sharing enjoyment and sadness through active involvement in relationships with friends," and "Sharing thoughts with friends and understanding what friends are thinking." No direction is given for pedagogical strategies teachers should use to reach these curricular goals. Nothing is mentioned about such practical considerations as what to do when children cry or fight. Koseirōdōshō's guidelines for *hoikuen* are much the same.

By describing the MEXT and Koseirōdōshō approaches as "hands-off" and "not directed from above," we do not mean to give the impression that guidelines for preschool issued by these ministries provide no guidance to preschools. The guidelines issued by both MEXT and Koseirōdōshō state a clear philosophy, and both agencies provide workshops and professional development. *The Kindergarten Education Guidelines* document issued by MEXT in 2002 is neither ambiguous nor equivocating. Just the opposite, it presents a consistent philosophy of early childhood education that has been articulated by MEXT for more than sixty years (Akita 2010; Nakatsubo et al. 2009). Unlike the U.S. government with "No Child Left Behind" and the National Association of Early Childhood Education with "Developmentally Appropriate Practice," MEXT does not give a name to their approach. And yet the *Guidelines* presents a consistent philosophy, one that we can call child-centered and play-based and that Japanese preschool directors and early childhood education experts call *nobi nobi kyōiku* ("room to stretch" or "feel at ease"), or *jiyū asobi* (free play). The Koseirōdōshō guidelines for *hoikuen* put forward a similar goal and a similar pedagogical approach. The MEXT and Koseirōdōshō guidelines do not provide specific standards or learning outcomes, as do the guidelines that govern early childhood education in many countries. MEXT and Koseirōdōshō have mechanisms for evaluating the fidelity with which schools and teachers are implementing their guidelines, but these are self-monitoring systems that carry no sanctions. The approach from the ministries is not to force preschools to follow government guidelines, but rather to encourage them to do so in their own way.

THE NONSPECIFICITY OF THE GUIDELINES AS A FORM OF *MIMAMORU*

Yutaka Oda and Mari Mori (2006) suggest that there has been a long struggle between those who want the kindergarten guidelines to be more like elementary school guidelines, in being specific about learning outcomes and broken down by content areas, and those who argue for less specific guidelines that would emphasize child development over content knowledge and skill, an approach championed by Sozo Kurahashi (1886–1955), the founding father of Japanese early childhood education. Kiyomi Akita (2010) suggests that the Japanese early childhood education curriculum reflects core ideas that can be traced back to Kurahashi's slogan: "For children's every-day life, in children's everyday life, and to children's everyday life." Akita explains that Kurahashi's philosophy emphasizes the importance of culti-vating young children's feelings, interests, and motivations by providing a supportive, stimulating environment. Oda and Mori credit Kurahashi with successfully opposing pressure in the prewar period to make more academi-cally oriented guidelines for preschools:

> At the time, some educators argued that the guidelines should be called *Yōchien Gakushu Shidō Yōryō* ("Kindergarten Course of Study"). The title, however, was not adopted. The term *Yōryō* (Guidelines) was used, reflecting the belief that because young children develop dif-ferently from one another, and because of their incomplete develop-ment, practice should emphasize their natural, everyday lives." (Oda and Mori 2006, 372)

The nondirectiveness of the *Guidelines* allows each preschool to develop its own pedagogical culture and gives the directors and their staff the ability to develop curriculum approaches that make sense for their local communi-ties. Ishigaki (1999) emphasizes kindergartens' autonomy:

> Each kindergarten should maintain its originality and make suit-able adjustments to its curriculum in accordance with the law and the *Guidelines*, responding to the mental and physical development of children, and the conditions of the kindergarten and local commu-nity. (26)

Sakiko Takeda, a preschool director in Tokyo, shared with us her appre-ciation for MEXT's nondirective policy approach:

> HAYASHI: Are you happy to have such a short curriculum guide?
> TAKEDA: I think the short curriculum means that MEXT is saying to us, "Please follow at least these things, and the rest is up to you." As a result, while compulsory education is almost the same every-where, early childhood education is highly varied. The *Guidelines* is in a way a bible that directors and preschool teachers interpret on their own.

Figure 6.2. Taro Machiyama, Tomoko Kumagai, Takaya Nogami, and Ritsuko Kumagai.

Takeda's explanation implies that by giving only minimal guidance, MEXT gives preschool directors and teachers latitude to develop their own approaches and, as a result, to take more responsibility for implementing the spirit of the guidelines.

The four preschool directors we interviewed in a focus group (figure 6.2) made a distinction between the government's approach to "hard" and "soft" domains of early childhood education. Hard domains include health policies (e.g., hygiene, food safety), space (playground and classroom square meters per child), and time (number of days of school each year and hours in each day). The soft domains are curriculum and pedagogy. As Director Machiyama put it: "They give us guidance for how to deal with the hard domains. The inside stuff they leave to us [nakami wa omakase]." Director Ritsuko Kumagai emphasized that MEXT provides only broad directions for the curriculum, which each preschool then has to operationalize:

> We follow the general guidelines. But each preschool has its own approach, its own way of interpreting the guidelines and turning them into practice. Look, I can show you our monthly and weekly and daily curriculum plans for each grade. These five terms in the first column come from the MEXT *Guidelines*: Health, Relationships, Environment, Language, Expression/Art. And we have added one more: Plants. For each of these areas, the MEXT *Guidelines* give just a broad definition, and then it is up to us to figure out what to do with it.

We asked the four directors: "Do the *Guidelines* specifically mention *mimamoru?*"

KUMAGAI: No, the word *mimamoru* isn't there. But I would say that the MEXT *Guidelines* have an atmosphere of *mimamoru*. There is more there than the literal meaning of the words. The document says a lot, but also leaves much unsaid. It has an atmosphere.

MACHIYAMA: There is not the term *mimamoru*, but it has the spirit of "Let's do *mimamoru* education."

KUMAGAI: Aren't our politics amazing? People in the ministries trust us. They have a big, open mind [literally, "a big bowl"], and they rely on us. This guideline is really well done. There are detailed hard aspects and then for the rest, they trust us. The book has a mood of *mimamoru*.

Director Kumagai then went to the bookshelves in the teachers' office of her *yōchien* where we were meeting, and returned with a set of books she placed on the table, books including the "hard" guidelines for health, safety, and architecture, a short curriculum guide, and a longer book, *Yōchien Kyōiku Yōryō Kaisetsu* (Interpreting the Preschool Curriculum). Director Kumagai said she finds this longer book very helpful. When we asked if it provided specific instructions for how to deal with situations such as children's fights or if it mentioned *mimamoru*, she replied, "Not at all." Director Machiyama agreed, explaining: "This book doesn't use the term *mimamoru*, but the book itself embodies the spirit of *mimamoru*. It doesn't say specifically what to do but instead requires us to work to find our own message in the book." We interpret Machiyama and Kumagai's comments here as praise for the restraint on the part of the book's authors and MEXT in not dictating practice, much as preschool teachers restrain the impulse to intervene in children's fights.

Several of the preschool directors we interviewed used the term "trust" to describe how the ministries deal with them. As Director Kumagai simply put it: "They trust us." This comment mirrors the comments of preschool teachers who explained their use of a strategy of *mimamoru* with such phrases as: "We trust children, so we can wait" and "We believe in children, so we can wait."

The nondirectiveness of the *Guidelines* supports as well as reflects the strength of preschool administrators. The majority of Japanese preschools are private programs (MEXT, 2009), with strong, long-serving directors who also often own the preschool. In public preschools, the power of directors comes from the fact that they are government employees with job stability who, while moving over the course of their careers from school to school, stay in the field for many years. In both types of programs, the looseness of the guidelines empowers directors and in this way allows for stability and for resisting calls from politicians and parents for a more academic curriculum.

The fact that there are specific guidelines for primary schools in Japan raises the question, Why not for preschools? One possible explanation is that *mimamoru* is a cultural practice that while found across many domains of Japanese society, is particularly well suited to *yōchien*, which historically and in the present day see their mission as primarily one of children's social and emotional development. The Japanese preschools' central goal is to make Japanese children Japanese (Tobin, Hsueh, and Karasawa 2009). This goal is seen as best achieved using "natural" means, which take the form of providing a social world where children can experience a level of social complexity missing in their circumscribed, closely supervised lives in contemporary Japan.

In their 2006 paper, Oda and Mori emphasize the significance of the choice by Japanese early childhood policymakers to use the term "education guideline" rather than "course of study." Most early childhood practitioners and policymakers reject the term "course of study," which they feel is too school-like. They prefer the term *kyōiku*, which is usually translated into English as "education," but which carries a meaning that goes well beyond schooling and the acquisition of academic knowledge. As a *yōchien* director in Kyoto explained to us: "The term *kyō* in *kyōiku* refers to education. But it is important to remember that *kyōiku* also has within it the term *iku*, which means 'to cultivate.'" The decision by MEXT to use the term "education guidelines" rather than "course of study" for kindergartens acknowledges that the central goal of early childhood education is social and emotional development, and not only education narrowly defined. Preschool in Japan is seen primarily as a site for children to become happy, socially well adjusted, and Japanese. Policy guidelines for education issued for primary and secondary schools in Japan and for pre-K through secondary education in many countries are usually concerned with how to achieve mathematics and literacy goals, and not about such "softer things" as enculturation, social and emotional development, and the development of the self.

A related cultural explanation for our observation that we can find *mimamoru* operating in *yōchien* policy as well as in practice would be that there is a metonymic linkage between Japanese early childhood education and Japanese childhood. Japanese early childhood education places a strong value on "childlikeness" (*kodomo rashii*) (Hoffman 1995) and the freedom to be childish, which means free to play, to explore nature, and to experience a range of emotions. As Diane Hoffman (2000) writes: "It is somewhat misleading to speak of child *development* in Japanese education—because the emphasis is on the child remaining true to her or his childlike nature rather than throwing off childlike characteristics in favor of attaining adult modes of being and functioning as soon as possible" (195). The term *yōchien* (幼稚園) contains the Chinese character for "garden." The term "children's garden" carries with it in Japanese, as in the original German term "kindergarten," the notion of a place that is free and natural. Just as kindergartens should be natural and free and allow children to explore, ministries regulating preschool should allow teachers and directors a similar freedom.

THE CASE OF DEAF PRESCHOOLS

Having consistently found in Japanese preschools a low intervention approach by teachers and minimal policy direction from government ministries, we were surprised when we began our research in Japanese schools for the deaf to find the opposite pattern: high intervention by teachers in classrooms and specific direction on curriculum and pedagogy from above. We suggest that Japanese teachers, directors, and policymakers follow an approach of low intervention unless and until there is a compelling reason to intervene. In this section we argue that deaf public preschools in Japan are a site where teachers, directors, and policymakers feel compelled to intervene. An understanding of why high intervention is felt to be necessary in public deaf schools makes clearer how and why low intervention functions in hearing preschools. In this section we contrast the high intervention practices of the public deaf preschools in Japan with the low intervention approaches followed both in hearing preschools and at Meisei Gakuen, the only school for the deaf in Japan that uses Japanese Sign Language (JSL) as the primary language of instruction and social interaction. We include Meisei in our analysis to show that it is possible to do deaf early childhood education in Japan without high intervention.

Unlike Meisei, the other 110 schools for the deaf in Japan, all of which are public, employ "total communication," a mixture of cued speech, finger spelling, lip-reading, and signed spoken Japanese. At Meisei, the preschool class of twelve three- to five-year-old children and their three teachers, two of whom are deaf, communicate entirely in JSL. In contrast, there are only a few preschool teachers at the public preschools who are deaf and only a few who are fluent in JSL, and the only children who are fluent have learned to sign not at school but at home, as "native signers" who are children of deaf signing parents.

At Meisei, as at Komatsudani and other hearing preschools we have studied, we find an emphasis on the development of emotions, on childlikeness, and on the value of teacher's strategic nonintervention in children's disputes. Our argument in this chapter is that the similarity of practices we find among teachers with such different backgrounds is due to the influence of professional practices that are widely shared, but implicit. *Mimamoru* is among a set of Japanese preschool practices that are implicit in the sense that they are not mandated by the Ministry of Education, systematically taught in teacher preparation programs, or found in textbooks. Instead they are passed down through on-the-job learning, reflective of national professional teaching cultures, and embedded in the larger culture and society in which schools are located. What needs explaining, then, is not why Ikeda and the other teachers at Meisei have a pedagogical approach that is much like the approach of teachers in hearing preschools, but instead why the teachers in the public deaf preschools do not, generally, follow this emic approach.

INTERVIEWS IN THE PUBLIC SCHOOLS FOR THE DEAF

We showed the subtitled video we made of a day in the preschool class at Meisei to teachers and administrators in schools for the deaf in four cities in Japan: Nara, Yokosuka, Chiba, and Sapporo. Participants at first were hesitant to comment, mostly, we think, out of reluctance to say something critical about another deaf school, and also because they found Meisei's approach so unlike their own that it was difficult to know what to say. As the director of one of the public deaf preschool programs said at the beginning of the interview: "It is totally different from our approach, because they use only JSL and we use total communication."

When we asked specifically for reactions to the tug-of-war scene, the most common response was to say that this approach was one they would follow if they were teaching students who shared a common language, as do the signing students at Meisei. For example, a teacher at Sapporo School for the Deaf commented: "If I were there, I would do the same thing as Ikeda-sensei." A teacher at the Yokosuka School for the Deaf said:

> I think this teacher can wait because children are able to communicate with each other without a teacher. Because we have both children who use oral language and children who use sign, we often have to intervene in children's interactions. We, too, do not want to interrupt children, but it's difficult to do that here.

An administrator at the Nara Deaf School said that Ikeda's nonintervention approach in the tug-of-war fights was good, but it is an approach that would not be feasible or desirable at her school:

> I cannot do it here because I need to be a mediator between two children because each child has a different level of language ability and a different way to communicate. As a teacher, we first need to make sure that children understand each other.

A teacher at the Chiba School for the Deaf commented on the tug-of-war scene:

> If I were in that situation, my thinking would be that I would want to trust them. It's important to let them solve their problem on their own. But sign is a language that we need to keep watching. When some children sign, I wonder if other children can share in their conversation. And do they keep other children waiting?

The similarities of these comments across the public deaf school sites suggest that they share with Ikeda and the teachers at the hearing preschools a belief in the value of nonintervention, but that they face barriers in putting this belief into practice in their school because of their students' lack of a common language and lack of language fluency. The total communication approach followed by the public deaf schools means not just that teachers use multiple modalities to communicate with children, but also that there is no single language of interaction, no lingua franca, among children. Teachers in our focus groups in the public deaf schools explained that they feel a need to mediate interactions among their students to compensate for the fact that they are working in a multilingual environment. Many of the teachers explained that their interventions most often take the form of providing interpretation among speaking, signing, and gesturing students, and in this way encouraging children to interact with peers, with the goal of helping deaf children move toward eventually being able to handle disputes and other social interactions on their own.

In addition to their students' lack of a common language, another rationale the educators in the public deaf programs gave for intervening in children's social interactions was that these students need a teacher to facilitate their interactions. The implication here is that because deaf children experience language delays, many also have cognitive and social-emotional delays in their development, delays that require more teacher intervention than is the case for hearing children. For example, an expert on deaf education at the National Institute of Special Needs Education emphasized the need to adjust pedagogy to the unique developmental needs of deaf children:

The crucial thing for deaf children is the ability to make predictions. For example, people cry not only because they are sad, but also when they are happy. A teacher can use picture cards, or write words in a notebook, to help the child understand what is happening. Teachers of the deaf need to have a variety of techniques to get children's attention and a variety of techniques to teach one simple word. They need to use their ears as well as their bodies, especially with young children.

By "ears" and "bodies" we assume that he is suggesting that by responding only with signing, Ikeda was missing an opportunity to engage with deaf children using the full range of communication modalities.

Behind this insistence on the need to facilitate multiple modalities of language development with deaf children is a belief that deaf children need to be taught to communicate in oral Japanese for preparation for life in the wider (nondeaf) Japanese society: "If you only sign, you can't communicate with your grandparents or neighbors." "If you can't speak, you can't ever get an office job." "Signing is fine for communicating with other deaf people who know Japanese Sign Language, but it is of no use for living in the wider world where people don't know sign." One experienced deaf educator went so far as to suggest: "It is morally wrong for parents or teachers to make the decision to teach young children only sign, because this decision takes away the children's right to learn how to speak." Another commented:

> When they [the Meisei students] go to high school and college, these children will have limited choices. They could go to Gallaudet, in America. However, when they come back, even if they have the ability, they won't be able to become a teacher. Well, I guess they could become a teacher at Meisei.

In some of the focus-group discussions in the public deaf preschools, teachers and directors suggested that they do not have the luxury their counterparts have in hearing preschools of holding back and letting language and social-emotional development emerge "naturally," because for deaf children oral language acquisition is not natural. This leads to an urgency to intervene and encourage communication to help deaf children catch up with their hearing peers as soon as possible, ideally in time for them to be mainstreamed for primary school. The urgency felt by the public school educators leads them to prioritize language acquisition over social-emotional development, or rather to see oral language development as a precursor to social-emotional development.

Meisei educators avoid this discourse of deaf students' need to catch up by centering their program on JSL rather than on helping deaf children acquire the ability to speak and understand speech. For deaf Japanese children, sign is their natural language, which like spoken Japanese for hearing Japanese children can be learned without didactic instruction, simply by immersing children in a language-rich environment (Stokoe 1980). At Meisei there is no more concern that children will not learn to sign than there is at hearing preschools that children will not learn to speak. In contrast, there is nothing natural about deaf children's learning to speak. It is a laborious project that requires ongoing technical interventions (Valente 2010).

As a result of this felt urgency to intervene, teachers in the public programs appear busier and more attentive to children than are Ikeda and her colleagues at Meisei. This can explain in part why the public deaf educators perceive Ikeda as failing to take advantage of teachable moments: the public school deaf educators in our focus groups tended to equate teachers' level of intervention and busyness with their professionalism and the quality of their teaching (Sharp and Green 1975). We observed an extreme contrast between Ikeda's "quietness" and reluctance to intervene and the busyness of teachers in the public deaf programs, who are constantly holding up flashcards, pointing to visual aids, using icons, finger spelling, mouthing words, repeating them, and scurrying around the classroom to intervene in interactions among children.

We think that the educators in the public deaf school begin with a different underlying core assumption about educational goals for deaf children. This different beginning assumption leads these teachers to turn away from *mimamoru* and other implicit pedagogical practices followed at Meisei and at hearing preschools and instead to use practices that reflect the logic and worldview of special education, of MEXT's approach to deaf education, and of larger Japanese cultural beliefs that all children, deaf as well as hearing, should be able to participate in the larger Japanese society.

Teachers and directors in the public deaf schools have not arrived at these views on their own. They receive much more in-service training and more explicit directives from experts at MEXT than do their counterparts in the private and public hearing programs. Approximately 50 percent of the teachers in the public deaf school have received a certificate of completion of formal training in deaf education, whereas it is very rare for teachers in the hearing preschools to complete an in-service training program. This is in part a question of numbers: there are only 110 deaf public preschools, as compared with over 5,000 hearing public preschools, so the staff at the deaf schools are visited far more frequently by experts and more often have a chance to attend in-service training.

We suggest that teachers and administrators working in the public deaf schools receive more direct training and guidance not only because their numbers are small, but also because both they and the experts providing training believe that the intuitive, low-intervention approach that is tacitly encouraged for hearing children is inadequate for deaf children. They believe deaf children require high-intervention, nonintuitive, specialized approaches that must be systematically taught and learned in preservice and in-service training. They therefore turn away from the intuitive logic that we have suggested guides practice in hearing preschools, and placing deaf children in the category of children with special needs, they turn to special education and speech therapy for pedagogical strategies.

We do not mean to suggest that there is not variation in the beliefs and approaches of the teachers working in the deaf public school. We suggest that these teachers are pulled in two directions—one the intuitive cultural logic that favors low intervention, the other the professional logic of special education that favors high intervention. Our observations in the deaf public schools suggest that some of these educators are on the low-intervention end of the continuum, intervening in their students' interactions to the minimum degree necessary, with most of their interventions taking the form of interpretation and facilitation of conversation. In contrast, public deaf school educators on the high-intervention end of the continuum frequently intervene in children's peer interactions to urge them to pronounce words intelligibly, even if this intervention interrupts the flow of the event. Those deaf educators toward the middle of this continuum forge hybrid practices, intervening to support cognitive and social-emotional as well as language development, and view their interventions as a step toward enabling the children to handle such social interactions on their own. A visible manifestation of this variety of viewpoints and approaches is that in some of the public deaf programs we visited, we observed children spending most of the day in peer interactions, with some mediation by teachers, while in other programs the children spent most of the day in adult-child dyadic interactions, emphasizing oral language development.

STRONG AND WEAK MATCHES OF BELIEFS, PRACTICES, AND POLICIES

We suggest that Meisei's approach is consistent with the implicit Japanese pedagogical practices, including *mimamoru*, found in the hearing preschools. In contrast, at the public deaf preschools, the priority placed on learning to pronounce words over the content of what is being said, on language acquisition over social development, and on adult-child over child-child interactions produces a tension between their pedagogical approach and implicit Japanese pedagogies of early childhood education.

This supports the thesis that within a nation, schools can be placed on a continuum that runs from a good match to a significant mismatch of their classroom practices with explicit educational policies and guidelines; implicit cultural beliefs and practices of teachers; and more general cultural values and larger social discourses.

Meisei's preschool program has a close match with Japanese implicit pedagogical practices, explicit national guidelines for preschool education (but not for deaf education), and larger Japanese cultural beliefs and practices. In the public deaf preschools, in contrast, there is a mismatch between their specialized pedagogical approach on the one hand, and the national kindergarten guidelines for "regular" early childhood education and Japanese implicit cultural pedagogical beliefs and practices on the other.

The result is a paradox: Meisei preschool, despite the fact that everyone there communicates only in JSL, feels very Japanese, while the total communication preschools feel less typically Japanese. Or we can state this thesis as an irony: The Japanese public deaf preschools that emphasize speaking and hearing and have as their central aim the eventual integration of deaf children into wider Japanese society may be less successful at helping these children become culturally and socially like their peers in hearing preschools than is the seemingly separatist signing school (Meisei), where the children develop socially, emotionally, and culturally much as they do in hearing schools, and where teachers teach much as their counterparts do in hearing schools, following a pedagogy of *mimamoru*.

The public deaf schools struggle with a parallel contradiction at the level of policy. Deaf education in Japan is defined as a subcategory of special education, and falls under the domain of the special education division of MEXT. In approaching the problem of how to structure services for deaf children as well as other categories of children needing accommodations not available in the regular schools, MEXT is caught between competing cultural values. Special education calls for the identification of difference, differentiated instructional approaches, and individualized attention, which is awkward in a nation that emphasizes the value of inclusion, homogeneity, and equality, not of opportunity, as in the United States, but of treatment (Maret 2008). Meisei, in contrast, uses a pedagogical approach that avoids discourses of special education, diagnosis, and intervention.

Meisei's approach is hardly a comfortable solution, however, as it is out of synch with other Japanese national values, discourses, and customs. In the United States, schools that emphasize Deaf cultural identity and sign language are supported by a wider cultural discourse of hyphenated identity and multiculturalism that makes possible not just a deaf university like Gallaudet, but also historically black and tribal colleges. In contrast, Meisei's emphasis on JSL and Deaf cultural identity is seen as divisive in a nation that is uncomfortable with identity politics and averse to multicultural education (Nakamura 2006).

We see the workings of implicit cultural beliefs and practices across levels of Japanese early childhood education. The kindergarten teacher hesitating to intervene in her students' disputes, the director giving her teachers latitude, and MEXT being nondirective with preschools all can be seen as examples of the same implicit cultural logic: the belief that directors, teachers, and students should be encouraged to find their own solutions. When teachers, supervisors, and policymakers hold back and use *mimamoru* (watching and waiting), rather than a more directive management style, the students or employees in their charge take more responsibility and are more motivated.

Cultural pedagogies that are implicit in the sense of not appearing in government guidelines or being taught in schools of education nevertheless play a significant part in a nation's teaching practices. These implicit practices, however, are vulnerable to being supplanted when teachers find themselves confronted with a situation such as the education of deaf children where, lacking confidence in these implicit pedagogies, they turn instead to more explicit, specialized approaches, such as those they import from the fields of special education and speech therapy.

Chapter 7

—

Reassembling the Cultural

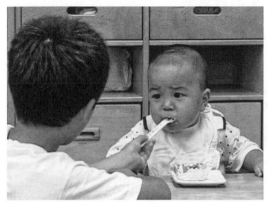

Figure 7.1.

A WORLD IN A SPOONFUL OF PUDDING

At Komatsudani Hoikuen each day after lunch, five children from the oldest class of five-year-olds put on aprons and go downstairs to help care for the infants and toddlers. Ken sits at the low table next to eleven-month-old Masaki and feeds him his snack of bread pudding. When Ken pushes the spoon too far into Masaki's mouth, Masaki quietly protests by pulling back his head and grimacing, and then turns to look toward Kawai-sensei, sitting just behind him. The teacher acknowledges Masaki's concern with a nod, and the spoon-feeding continues (figure 7.2a–c).

There is a whole world of meaning in these thirty seconds. To do justice to the complexity of this interaction, we need to attend microscopically to the second-by-second interactions of the big boy, smaller one, and the teacher, and at the same time to attend macroscopically to the larger context in which this scene plays out.

To understand the cultural specificity of this scene we must pay close attention to what is communicated, symbolically, by each grimace, smile, and gesture. A microanalysis of the scene shows Ken experimenting with just

Figure 7.2a. Masaki pulls back.

Figure 7.2b. Looking toward his teacher.

Figure 7.2c. Feeding continues.

how far and how hard he should push the spoon into Masaki's mouth. When the spoon goes in too far, Masaki pulls back his head and grimaces, but both the movement and the facial expression are subtle, perhaps just enough to communicate to Ken that he needs to ease up on the spoon, but not so strong a reaction as to bring the interaction to a halt. After that spoonful of pudding has been transferred from spoon to mouth, Masaki, while chewing, turns his head to his teacher, who nods slightly and smiles, gestures we interpret as meant both to reassure Masaki that everything is fine and to remind Ken not to push too hard on the spoon. To understand this scene we need to attend not just to what Kawai did do, but also to what she refrained from doing. For example, if at the moment when Ken pushed too hard on the spoon she had intervened verbally, telling him to be careful, the interaction could have taken a different turn, with both older and younger boys losing confidence and as a result perhaps giving up. Japanese educators who commented on the scene generally liked everything about the interaction with the exception of the use here of a stiff, large spoon, where a more pliable, smaller, softer one would have been preferable.

We also need to consider how some factors that are not visible, but still present, have an impact on the participants' actions. Some Japanese early childhood educators who watched this scene suggested that such mixed-age interactions are especially valuable in an era in Japan when the birthrate is so low that many older children do not have younger siblings, and therefore lack opportunities at home to develop *omoiyari* (empathy). A *yōchien* director commented wistfully that opportunities such as this one for an older boy to care for a baby are possible in *hoikuen* (daycare centers) like Komatsudani, but not in kindergartens, where there are no children younger than three years old. Some U.S. teachers who watched this scene worried that five-year-olds are too young to care for babies, and wondered if Masaki's parents were aware that the care of their baby during part of the day was being turned over to a five-year-old. When we conveyed this concern to the staff at Komatsudani, they told us that parents know that mixed-age interaction is a daily feature of their program, appreciate this family-like arrangement, and trust both the teachers and the older children to keep their children safe.

For heuristic reasons, we have broken this book into chapters, each of which has dealt with a separate topic: feelings, fighting, peripheral participation, adjusting bodily demeanor, teaching expertise, and early childhood education policy. A cost of such a presentation is a loss of the interconnectedness of these issues. Children do not learn about feelings on Mondays and how to use their bodies on Tuesdays; teachers do not teach children about literacy at ten o'clock and social skills at eleven; rather, it all happens at once. The goal of this concluding chapter is to reassemble the factors that contribute to the richness of life in Japanese preschools by presenting analyses of events that combine the themes we have to this point treated separately. For example, we can see Ken's feeding of Masaki as combining empathy, *mimamoru, kejime*, the gallery (in this case, their teacher and the other babies nearby), early childhood education and care policy, and societal notions of risk and the need for children to experience mixed-age play.

THINKING ABOUT CULTURE

Our central concern has been the contribution of cultural factors to life in Japanese preschool classrooms. The goal of the preceding chapters was to identity, describe, and analyze the workings of what we call the implicit and tacit cultural dimensions of Japanese preschool pedagogy. Our argument is not that culture explains *every* thing that happens in preschool classrooms, just that culture can explain *some* things. Or to put it another way: among the factors that interact to produce classroom practices we need to consider culture.

In this concluding chapter we consider the relationship between cultural and other factors. But that statement is not quite right, because it implies that some factors are cultural and others are not. We need to move beyond such binary categorizations and see the inherent interpenetration and interplay of the social and the cultural. We need to consider how such dimensions of the social as bureaucratic, political, economic, and demographic factors press on cultural pedagogies and how these cultural pedagogies are never only cultural.

In this chapter we use aspects of Bruno Latour's actor network theory (ANT), as presented in his book *Reassembling the Social* (2005), but we do not aim to offer a Latourian analysis. One reason for shying away from calling our conceptual framework Latourian is that, as Latour points out, ANT is not, despite its misleading name, a theory; it's a method, one that is closest to ethnography and ethnomethodology, in privileging thick description over the a priori theorizing of causes. For this reason we prefer to describe our approach as a version of ethnography that is informed by the writings of Latour, Bourdieu, and other social theorists. The second reason we hesitate to present our argument as a form of ANT is that Latour, while praising anthropology as a method, is largely silent on the role of culture. We take our task, therefore, to be not to apply Latour, but instead to do a parallel project; just as Latour's goal is to reassemble the social, ours is to reassemble the cultural, which requires separating out actors and factors (which Latour calls "actants") before we can suggest how these actors and factors are connected.

Latour calls for a flattening, by which he means a nonhierarchicalizing, of the factors that interact to produce social life, and for avoiding an a priori privileging of any one factor over another as being more powerful or causal. In some cases, but not all, a directive from a ministry of education has more effect on practice in a classroom than does a teacher's intuition or bodily habitus or a child's emotional state. Whether a formal policy, an implicit pedagogical practice, or a child's mood will have more influence on a particular moment in a classroom cannot be known without careful empirical attention. More useful than ranking the relative strength of causal factors is attention to how causal factors interact.

THE TEDDY BEAR FIGHT REVISITED

In this final chapter we attempt a synthesis, but not a conclusion, in the sense of proposing one central theme that ties all the disparate parts together. As Latour (2005) writes: "Don't try to shift from description to explanation: simply continue the description" (70). We do so in this section by returning once more to the teddy bear fight at Komatsudani Hoikuen, this time showing that it is an example not only of *mimamoru*, but of how all the topics we talked about in each of the preceding chapters are present in this one event: feelings, *mimamoru*, *kejime*, embodiment, gallery, and policy. In the analysis that follows, we combine attention to teachers' intentions and implicit cultural pedagogical practices with attention as well to structures, routines, architecture, and things in the classroom. We bring in notions of contingency and emergence, arguing that, like the flapping of a butterfly's wings, one small factor can send an event off in a new direction.

Mimamoru

In chapter 1 we presented the teddy bear fight at Komatsudani as an example of how Morita and other Japanese teachers employ the Japanese pedagogical concept of *mimamoru* (observing and caring with minimal intervention). We call *mimamoru* an implicit cultural practice for several reasons: It's a strategy Morita and the two other Japanese teachers we videotaped and interviewed, Kaizuka at Madoka Yōchien and Ikeda at Meisei Gakuen, offered as an explanation for their holding back in children's fights. It was also mentioned by many other Japanese early childhood educators who watched our videos as a factor in their approach to classroom disagreements. While not all teachers said they would employ *mimamoru* as Morita did in the teddy bear fight, all found the logic familiar. We call *mimamoru* implicit because it is not mentioned in the Ministry of Education guidelines for kindergartens, covered in textbooks, or explicitly addressed in either preservice or in-service training.

In the video of the teddy bear fight we see little of Morita, who is busy with lunch preparation. We see her walk through the frame twice and at one point call out "Hey!" from across the room. Her degree of absence during an intense three-minute physical and verbal fight among the group of girls is evidence of her low intervention. The evidence that this low intervention is an example of *mimamoru* (and not, for example, of negligence) comes from Morita's post hoc explanation, as she both describes and justifies her nonintervention by citing the pedagogical practice of *mimamoru*. As Maurice Bloch (1991) reminds us, such a post hoc verbal explanation does not necessarily mean that at the moment she hesitated to intervene, Morita was consciously thinking of *mimamoru*. Nevertheless, Morita's citing of *mimamoru* is evidence that this construct is connected to her practice, or to put it in Latour's terms, that in this instance *mimamoru* is an actant, a causal factor that has left a trace. Moreover, the fact that so many of her counterparts working at other Japanese preschools also explain their practice using the concept of *mimamoru* is strong evidence for the power of this implicit cultural pedagogical concept.

A problem of this explanation is that while it is not wrong, it is incomplete, as it cuts off this cultural practice from other factors with which it interacts. In pointing out the centrality of *mimamoru* in Japanese preschool teaching in chapter 1, we did not intend to ascribe to *mimamoru* a unilateral or determining causal power. Instead, we see *mimamoru* as among the factors that influenced the outcome of the teddy bear fight and other events where Japanese teachers hold back from intervening. What are these other factors? And in what way can they be seen as interacting?

Techniques of the Body

While cognizant of the risk of proposing a mind/body duality, we suggest it is useful to consider how the teacher's body functions as an agent in itself. Teachers and practitioners in other fields often describe experiencing their bodies as both them and not them, or as another part of them than their conscious, intentional mind. Latour (2005) gives the example of a famous soprano who says, "It is my voice who tells me when to stop and when to begin" to raise the question of what sociologists (or in our case, anthropologists) are to do with such comments by expert practitioners:

> The soprano did say that she shared her life with her voice that made her do certain things. Are we able to treasure this odd way of speaking or not? It was very precise, very revealing, very telling, and also very moving. Is not being moved, or rather, put into motion by the informants exactly what we should mean by an enquiry? (48)

What are we to do with statements by Morita and other Japanese teachers that suggest that much of their practice, including *mimamoru*, they do without conscious premeditation? As we discussed in chapter 1, a teacher "does" *mimamoru* with her body by being optimally present to the children, appearing attentive enough so they know their fighting cannot go too far and inattentive enough so they know that the teacher is not about to jump in, and therefore that the responsibility for working out the disagreement is primarily on their shoulders. This artful performance of attention/inattention is what Mauss (1934/1973) calls a technique of the body; Bourdieu (2000) a bodily habitus; Polanyi (1966) tacit knowledge; and Bloch (1991) nonlinguistically coded knowledge that Japanese teachers have acquired without being explicitly taught and implement with increasing expertise as they gain years of experience.

Our microanalysis of Ikeda's performance of attention and inattention during the long tug-of-war fight is an example caught on video of such an embodied performance of *mimamoru* (figure 7.3a and b). When we asked Ikeda to reflect on her actions during this scene, she referred to the logic of nonintervention, but she also said that this concept was not consciously in her mind during the fight, and that her looking away at key junctures was something she did not consciously but rather "naturally." All three teachers we interviewed in depth used the words "natural" and "without thinking"

Figure 7.3a and b. Ikeda looks away as Mika and Satoshi argue and looks on as Chika makes a point to Satoshi.

to describe aspects of their teaching, much as accomplished soccer players talk about an especially skillful pass and sopranos about their soaring arias.

Expertise

A separation of the mind and body into separate loci of action is also implied in comments made to us by experienced teachers and directors who said that the key difference between beginning and expert teachers lies less in the pedagogical beliefs they hold than in their ability to put these beliefs into practice effectively. The early career Japanese preschool teachers we interviewed told us they believe in the value of *mimamoru* as a pedagogical practice. They just don't know how to "do" *mimamoru* artfully, to maximum effect. In other words, sometimes the mind and the body are not on the same page or at the same level of accomplishment.

In our follow-up interviews with Morita ten years after we videotaped the teddy bear fight, she discussed how she had changed. She described this earlier iteration of herself as clumsy, rushed, and too directive in her interactions with children. This comment reminds us that the video we shot in 2002 was Morita on a particular day, at a particular point in her career and development as a preschool teacher. Throughout this book we have referred to Japanese teachers' implicit cultural practices. But we should avoid seeing these practices as fixed. *Mimamoru* and other pedagogical practices feel to Japanese teachers to be both natural and habitual, but this does not mean they are unchanging. As Bourdieu (2000) writes: "Habitus change constantly in response to new experiences. Dispositions are subject to a kind of permanent revision" (161).

Previous Interactions

Figure 7.4. A previous teddy bear argument.

When we asked Morita about the teddy bear fight, she said, "That's recently been a routine activity for these girls." A shot from earlier in the day in the Komatsudani video captured a previous argument over the teddy bear among this same group of girls (figure 7.4). This comment suggests that the routineness of the fight informed Morita's nonintervention. If the girls had never before fought like this over a teddy bear, Morita might have been more concerned and therefore acted differently. If these girls had not fought like this many times before, this fight would have felt different to them and they would have acted differently. If the other children in the class had not seen such a fight before among these girls, they would have reacted to it differently. These children have not only individual histories, interests, and embodied strategies for navigating life in preschool, but also a collective history and established patterns of interaction. This means not that each new interaction exactly repeats an earlier one, but that early interactions lay down grooves that guide without determining the course for subsequent ones.

Nao's Baby Brother

In one of the last scenes of the Komatsudani video, at the end of the long schoolday, we see Nao meeting her mother and baby brother in the schoolyard (figure 7.5). We suggest that this infant is an actor in the teddy bear

Figure 7.5. Nao's baby brother.

fight, not because we believe, as outsiders, that his birth explains Nao's whiny behavior during the day we filmed, but because Morita told us that Nao had been having a hard time since her baby brother was born. Morita's explanation implies that her (non)response to the fight was informed by a theory of child development, a belief that children are stressed by the birth of a younger sibling, and therefore likely to be emotionally needy at this time. What counts here is not whether this theory is true, but that it is a belief that Morita reports as having an impact on her assessment of the fight and therefore her actions. Morita told us she would be more likely to intervene in a situation where she lacked an explanation for why a child was acting provocatively. We can say that Nao's baby brother had an impact on the teddy bear fight via the cultural belief that children regress emotionally when their mother has a baby.

A Box of Teddy Bears

Figure 7.6a and b. A box of teddy bears.

Latour suggests that we should consider the impact on events of nonhuman as well as human actors. We suggest that not only the teddy bear the girls fight over but also the teddy bears we can glimpse in a storage container in the background of the shot are also acting here. If there were just one teddy bear in the classroom, Morita, the girls, and we viewers would evaluate the situation differently. Whether we view a resource as scarce or abundant changes our sense of its value and its power to motivate action. As a teacher at another preschool said about this scene: "It seems at first like these girls are fighting over the teddy bear, but when we see the other bears in the background [figure 7.6a and b] we can realize that it's more of a game than a fight, more about playing [*jareau*] and social interaction." Morita supported this interpretation, as she told us that Nao was primarily interested not in the bear, but in having social interactions with this group of slightly older girls.

At one point in the argument Yoko says to Nao: "That's not your bear, Nao-chan, it's Seiko's." While we cannot claim to understand fully the complexity of the meanings of the bears in the girls' play, this comment suggests the possibility that the fight over the bear is less an argument about rules for sharing than a custody dispute. Within the frame of this ongoing dramatic play, the teddy bears seem to be cast in the role of babies. When the other girls admonish Nao for taking the bear, they may be accusing her of an act as inappropriate within the frame of their play as a mother's attempting to go home from daycare with someone else's child. This interpretation would suggest that they aren't telling Nao that she can't have a bear of her own, or teaching her about the importance of sharing and taking turns, but rather criticizing her for breaking the rules of the pretend play, in which the bears

Figure 7.7. Seiko (with her bear under her dress), Reiko
(holding her bear), and Yoko talk with Nao.

are infants. We are not sure if it supports or undermines this interpretation for us to point out that the girls slip their teddy bears under the fronts
of their dresses or t-shirts, an apparently maternal gesture, albeit one that
combines elements of pregnancy with carrying an infant. In figure 7.7, we
see one of the twins, Reiko, maternally cradling her bear, careful to support
his neck, while her twin sister, Seiko, has her bear nestled inside her dress.

The Piano

Figure 7.8a and b. Pianos.

Another nonhuman actor here is the piano we can see in the background
behind the fighting girls. Morita told us that she was keeping an eye on the
fight, and that at the moment she saw the girls wrestling close to the corner of the piano (figure 7.8a), she made her only intervention, by calling out
"Kora, kora" (Hey!). In other words, the sharp corner of the piano (figure

7.8b) acted here not because one of the children bumped into it, but because Morita's concern led her to call out.

This explanation highlights the contingent nature of classroom life and preschool pedagogy. Morita is generally guided by the cultural concept of *mimamoru* and by a bodily habitus that leads her during times of free play in the classroom to keep an eye on children without intervening. Had the girls during the peak of their physical fighting over the teddy bear not ventured toward the sharp edge of the piano, Morita would not have called out to them to be careful. Had they moved even closer to the sharp corner, Morita would have done more than just call out "Hey."

Morita's level of concern about the corner of the piano has to do not only with sharp edges and fragile foreheads, but also with her sense of risk. A situation that in one culture would be deemed too risky for nonintervention might be considered tolerable in another (Burke and Duncan 2015, 81–82).

The Gallery

Figure 7.9a–c. Children come close to look and listen as their classmates fight and talk.

During the teddy bear fight we can see several other children approach the fighting girls (figure 7.9a–c). Maki, in the long, patterned dress, observes the beginning of the struggle, makes an attempt to intervene, and then gives up and watches from a distance. Toshi, in his number 6 jersey, at one point approaches the girls to listen to and observe the argument from close range. Mina, in tic-tac-toe patterned t-shirt, comes near Nao and Yoko to witness the denouement of the fight. We tend not to notice these onlookers because we jump to a conclusion about who the protagonists are in the scene. As we discussed in chapter 3, these onlookers are also participants who affect the meaning of this event by serving as a concerned audience, who may have a moderating (or escalating) effect on the fighting girls' behavior.

Architecture

Architecture is another factor that has an impact on preschool classroom dynamics. The relatively small size of Morita's classroom acts as a factor in the teddy bear fight by making physical interactions more likely and by removing oneself from contact with others more difficult. The absence of any tall furniture or dividers in the classroom acts to encourage eye contact among children and between children and the teacher. The sliding doors that divide Morita's classroom from the one adjoining were wide open during the fight, which we can speculate gave Morita more latitude to leave the room, knowing that Nogami next door could hear and see what was going on in her classroom (figure 7.10). Morita told us years later that having the more experienced Nogami teaching next door gave her an increased sense of security. In this sense we can say that Nogami was doing *mimamoru* with (watching over) Morita, which in turn made it easier for Morita to do *mimamoru* with her students.

Guidelines

Large student/teacher ratios affect social relations in Japanese classrooms by increasing the number of potential interpersonal interactions among children (figure 7.11). The student/teacher ratio of twenty or more children to one teacher also makes it more difficult for a Japanese teacher to closely monitor and mediate children's behavior than in a preschool system, such as that of the United States, with much smaller student/teacher ratios. Student/teacher ratios and other policies interact in complex ways with cultural practices—we cannot say that one determines the other. We should also not think of policy and cultural practices as opposing forces, because policy is also in part cultural (Hayashi 2011). The thirty children to one teacher ratio for preschools set by the Japanese government ministries that oversee daycare centers and kindergartens reflects many factors: it is in part economic, in part historical, and in part a reflection of an implicit cultural belief in the value of large classes with a high student/teacher ratio to encourage the development of a sense of community among children.

When the teddy bear fight broke out, Morita was busy cleaning up the

Figure 7.10. Sliding doors open between adjoining classrooms.

Figure 7.11. Morita serves tea to her class of 22 four-year-olds.

classroom before lunch and helping children finish changing out of their swimsuits back into their clothes. She had to perform these custodial tasks — chores that we suggest have the effect of making intervention in children's disputes less likely—because in Japan (unlike China, for example) most preschool teachers work without the help of an aide.

While government guidelines do not directly cause or always predict the practice of teachers, they help to create a context in which children and teachers act and interact. The guidelines for preschools of the Ministry of Education and the Ministry of Welfare have an emphasis on children's social development that is consistent with Morita's explanation of her nonintervention as a strategy for encouraging children to experience and handle social interactions on their own. In chapter 6 we suggested that the absence of explicit directions for how to handle fights among children has the effect of giving Japanese teachers latitude that teachers lack in many other systems.

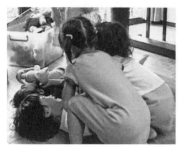

Figure 7.12a–c. Coordinated physical interactions among the fighting girls.

In contrast, in the Guidelines for Deaf Education, more specific direction contributes to more aggressive interventions by teachers in children's inter- actions in the public deaf preschools. We are suggesting not that these guide- lines determine classroom practice, but that they are grooves that pedagogy flows in.

Intercorporeality

To appreciate the complexity of an event such as the teddy bear fight re- quires that we pay attention not only to the protagonists' individuals ac- tions, but also to the coordination and interconnectedness of the bodies in the classroom. The concept of intercorporeality as discussed by Erving Goff- man (1971) and Maurice Merleau-Ponty (1964) reminds us that life in a Japa- nese preschool classroom requires interconnected and harmonized bodies. We can see examples of intercorporeal synchronicity in the teddy bear fight (figure 7.12a–c). At first glance, the pile of girls pulling on the teddy bear and each other seems chaotic rather than coordinated, and intercorporeal only in the most literal sense of bodies being in physical contact. But a frame-by- frame analysis of the physical tussle over the bear and of the interactions that follow as the girls work out their argument shows a synchronization of coordinated bodies moving through time and space. The girls roll around on the floor, but no one gets hurt, suggesting that this was far from an out- of-control melee. To roll around in a multiperson pile without hitting some- one's face with a knee or elbow requires a control of one's own body and an awareness of the bodies of others. Throughout the five minutes it takes from the first grabbing of the bear to the pinkie shake and promise at the end, a gallery of children not directly involved in the dispute comes close to the key protagonists and then drifts away, indirectly participating without drawing attention to themselves and distracting the disputants. During the argument, as the girls vociferously make their points, they also artfully move their bodies through space and make good use of the classroom furniture and materials. Each of the girls arguing with Nao puts a teddy bear under her shirt or dress; Seiko not only puts the bear in dispute under her dress front but also goes under a table, making it more difficult for Nao to get at it. This is not the synchronized intercorporeality of a dance company or of marching soldiers, but more akin to the kind of coordination of bodies in spaces in Erving Goffman's description of commuters artfully avoiding each other on a busy city street, or to the way roommates learn to share a small apartment, as they come together and move apart throughout the day.

A child new to preschool takes some time to master the techniques of the body required during the flow of the schoolday. These bodily techniques include taking shoes on and off in the entranceway, engaging with various pieces of equipment and in various games on the playground, gathering in a group for morning opening and afternoon departure, washing up, using the toilets, and taking out and putting away lunch utensils. These bodily techniques require the coordination of each of these movements with those of teachers and classmates, a coordination that allows for physical connection in the form of standing and sitting shoulder to shoulder, touching hands and arms, and occasional physical fights that do not cause injury, as well as the avoidance of collisions and uncoordinated and unwelcome touches that would lead to a breakdown in the flow of activities, breakdowns like those Goffman describes when two pedestrians approaching on a sidewalk fail to negotiate right of way and end up momentarily face to face, unable to move. After a few months in a preschool class such awkward encounters become rare, and the smooth intercorporeal flow of bodies the norm. Nao, who had been at Komatsudani about five months when we made the video, knew for the most part how to participate in the intercorporeal flow of bodies, as well as how to negotiate the daily routines. Her fight with the girls did not constitute a breakdown of intercorporeal engagement or social play, but instead, as Morita suggested, was a successful version of involving her classmates in a complex, coordinated, social-intercorporeal interaction.

This analysis is consistent with our larger arguments that Japanese preschools are key sites in contemporary Japan for young children to learn to be social, which includes not just learning the rules and conventions of daily Japanese life, but also how to move one's body in familiar, intelligible ways and to coordinate one's movements with those of others in space.

Contingency and Emergence

Teachers' decisions about when to make a point of not being available to mediate a dispute, when to draw physically near to give support without actively intervening, and when to actively mediate, with words, touch, and gesture, reflect not a set of rules or even principles, but instead a complex calculation. Or perhaps "decision" and "calculation" are the wrong words here, as they imply a conscious process of thinking that we suspect is not always or even usually involved in determining how Japanese teachers come to act. The word "decision" places too much emphasis on conscious reflection and too little on emergent, contingent action.

Japanese preschool classrooms are good examples of what Spiro and his colleagues (2007) call "an ill-structured domain," in the sense that they require the teacher to juggle competing demands, such as a variety of routine tasks and one or more disputes at the same time. The complexity of demands on the teachers' time and attention in the Japanese preschool classroom means they continually need to make decisions about who needs what level of support and which situations require their proximity, which just a verbal reminder, and which their more active mediation. Or perhaps it is more accurate to say that Japanese teachers continuously adjust their location, gaze, and presence in the classroom, without necessarily going through a conscious decision-making strategy to do so.

We can describe Morita's practice in the teddy bear fight as emerging out of an assemblage of actors, things, structural characteristics of Japanese education, spatial and temporal contexts, pedagogical schema, and embodied practices, or more specifically: little girls, new baby brother, teddy bear, sharp piano edge, clothes-changing and lunch-preparation duties, student/teacher ratios, *mimamoru*, and distracted-yet-aware gaze. If one or more of these factors had not been present here, Morita's practice might have veered off in another direction, one that would be not random but reflective of the interaction of contextual factors with implicit cultural beliefs and practices and embodied teaching practices.

CULTURAL PRACTICES AS AFFORDING AND CONSTRAINING

A key argument of this book is that among the factors that influence classroom practices, we need to consider the role culture plays in pedagogical beliefs and practices. Emic practices provide affordances to Japanese teachers that are less available to teachers in other cultures. These Japanese cultural practices are among the items on the menu of possible pedagogical actions available to Japanese teachers.

Some of the practices of Japanese teachers and children found in Japanese preschools can also be seen in other domains of Japanese society; for example, the bodily techniques of bowing in different registers of formality to modulate interpersonal communications are not unique to school settings. Some cultural practices, such as *mimamoru*, can be observed in other Japanese settings, but not in the same form they take in preschools, leading us to describe *mimamoru* as a practice characteristic not of Japanese society as a whole, but of teachers as a subset of Japanese society who are members of "a national teaching culture" (Anderson-Levitt 2002).

Our videotaping and interviewing have allowed us to identify and analyze a set of pedagogical practices that are widely shared across Japanese preschools and a set of beliefs associated with these practices. Culture is not the only factor that can produce such consistencies; other contributing factors can include government guidelines, teacher preparation programs, and financial exigency (e.g., economic depression leading to reduced government spending on education and, as a result, higher student/teacher ratios). We have argued that Japanese preschool pedagogy is an ideal case for showing the workings of culture because we find practices being widely shared without being dictated from above, codified in textbooks or government guidelines, or responsive to any obvious economic or political pressure.

This book at heart has been an empirical study, based on close analyses of images and interviews. In advance of doing careful ethnographic research for a particular topic such as Japanese preschool teaching, we cannot make an a priori claim that culture is the best explanation, nor can we rule culture out as an explanation. It is a question not of belief or orientation, but instead of empirical analysis and thick description.

Acknowledgments

Portions of this work appeared earlier, in different form, in "The Japanese Hands-Off Approach to Curriculum Guidelines for Early Childhood Education as a Form of Cultural Practice," *Asian-Pacific Journal of Research in Early Childhood Education* 5, no. 2 (2011): 107–23; "The Pedagogy of Feeling: Cultural Strategies for Supporting Young Children's Emotional Development," *Ethos* 37, no. 1 (2011): 32–49; "The Japanese Preschool's Pedagogy of Peripheral Participation," *Ethos* 39, no. 2 (2011): 139–64; "Reframing a Visual Ethnography of a Japanese Preschool Classroom," *Visual Anthropology Review* 28, no. 1 (2012): 13–31; and "The Power of Implicit Teaching Practices: Continuities and Discontinuities in Pedagogical Approaches of Deaf and Hearing Preschools in Japan," *Comparative Education Review* 58, no. 1 (2014): 24–46. We appreciate the policy of these journals to allow authors to reuse material in books.

We would like to acknowledge the support of the Spencer Foundation, who funded both the Preschool in Three Cultures Revisited and the Deaf Kindergarten studies. We also offer our sincere appreciation to Nancy Eisenberg, David Berliner, and Gustavo Fischman for their insights; Kathryn Anderson-Levitt and Daniel Walsh for their formative feedback on earlier drafts of this manuscript; our acquisition editor, Elizabeth Branch Dyson, for her commitment to this project; and the editorial and design team at the University of Chicago Press and especially to Susan Tarcov for her copyediting and Isaac Tobin for the cover.

Finally, we thank the directors, teachers, and children of the preschools where we conducted fieldwork for this project. We are especially grateful for the assistance we received from the three preschools that served as our key research sites: Komatsudani Hoikuen, Madoka Yōchien, and Meisei Gakuen. We treasure our ongoing professional relationships with Komatsudani's Directors Hidenori and Hironori Yoshizawa, Head Teacher Takaya Nogami, and classroom teacher Chisato Morita; Madoka's Directors Yoshio and Taro Machiyama and classroom teacher Mariko Kaizuka; and Meisei's Directors Michio Saito and Yoko Kaya, administrative staff Norie Oka and Mami Wakabayashi, and classroom teacher Akiko Ikeda. We were also helped in our research by Directors Ritsuko and Tomoko Kumagai of Senzan Yōchien. Thank you all for not only helping us but also believing in us. We will repay your trust by continuing to conduct our research sincerely.

References

Abu-Lughod, L., & Lutz, C. (1990). Introduction: Emotion, Discourse, and the Politics of Everyday Life. In *Language and the Politics of Emotion*, ed. C. Lutz & L. Abu-Lughod, 1–23. Cambridge: Cambridge University Press.

Akiba, M. (2004). Nature and Correlates of Ijime—Bullying in Japanese Middle School. *International Journal of Educational Research* 41 (3): 216–36.

Akita, K. (2010). Recent Curriculum Reform in Japan: The Future of Everyday-Life-Oriented Curriculum. Presented at the International Conference of KSECE, Pusan.

Althusser, L. (1971). Ideology and Ideological State Apparatus. In *Mapping Ideology*, ed. S. Zizek. London: Verso.

Anderson-Levitt, K. (2002). *Teaching Cultures: Knowledge for Teaching First Grade in France and the United States (Language and Social Processes)*. Cresskill, NJ: Hampton.

Anderson-Levitt, K. (2012). Complicating the Concept of Culture. *Comparative Education* 48 (4): 441–54.

Anderson-Levitt, K. (2013). What Is "National Culture"—Not to Mention "World Culture"—If Cultural Meaning Is Locally Produced? Paper presented at the Comparative and International Education Society annual meeting, New Orleans, March 11.

Azuma, H. (1994). *Nihonjin no shituke to kyōiku*. Tokyo: Tokyo Daigaku Syupankai.

Bakhtin, M. (1982). *The Dialogic Imagination: Four Essays*. Trans. C. Emerson & M. Holquist. Austin: University of Texas Press.

Bakhtin, M. (1990). *Art and Answerability*. Trans. M. Holquist & V. Liapunov. Austin: University of Texas Press.

Ball, D., & Cohen, D. (1999). Developing Practice, Developing Practitioners: Toward a Practice-Based Theory of Professional Education. In *Teaching as the Learning Profession: Handbook of Policy and Practice*, ed. G. Sykes & L. Darling-Hammond, 3–32. San Francisco: Jossey-Bass.

Ben-Ari, E. (1996). From Mothering to Othering: Organization, Culture, and Nap Time in a Japanese Day-Care Center. *Ethos* 24 (1): 136–64.

Ben-Ari, E. (1997). *Body Projects in Japanese Culture: Culture, Organization and Emotions in a Preschool*. Richmond, UK: Curzon Press.

Bender, A., Spada, H., Seitz, S., Swoboda, H., & Traber, S. (2007). Anger and Rank in Tonga and Germany: Cognition, Emotion, and Context. *Ethos* 35 (2): 196–234.

Benedict, R. (1946). *The Chrysanthemum and the Sword: Patterns of Japanese Culture*. Boston: Meridian.

Berliner, D. C. (1988). *The Development of Expertise in Pedagogy*. AACTE Publications, 1 Dupont Circle, Suite 610, Washington, DC 20036-2412.

Bloch, M. (1991). Language, Anthropology and Cognitive Science. *Man*, n.s., 26 (2): 183–98.

Bourdieu, P. (2000). Bodily Knowledge. *Pascalian Mediations*. Palo Alto, CA: Stanford University Press.

Briggs, J. (1999). *Inuit Morality Play: The Emotional Education of a Three-Year-Old.* New Haven, CT: Yale University Press.

Burke, R., & Duncan, J. (2015). *Bodies as Sites of Cultural Reflection in Early Childhood Education.* New York and London: Routledge.

Caudill, W., & Plath, D. (1966). Who Sleeps by Whom? Parent-Child Involvement in Urban Japanese Families. *Psychiatry* 29: 344–66.

Clark, S. (1994). *Japan, a View from the Bath.* Honolulu: University of Hawaii Press.

Clark, S. (1998). Learning at the Public Bathhouse. In *Learning in Likely Places*, ed. J. Singleton, 239–52. New York: Cambridge University Press.

Connor, L., Asch, T., & Asch, P. (1986). *Jero Tapakan: Balinese Healer.* Cambridge: Cambridge University Press.

Conroy, M., Hess, R., Azuma, H., & Kashiwagi, K. (1980). Maternal Strategies for Regulating Children's Behavior. *Journal of Cross-Cultural Psychology* 11 (2): 153–72.

Crossley, N. (1995). Body Techniques, Agency and Intercorporeality: On Goffman's Relations in Public. *Sociology* 29 (1): 133–49.

Crossley, N. (2007). Researching Embodiment by Way of 'Body Techniques.' *Sociological Review* 55 (1): 80–94.

DeCoker, G. (1998). Seven Characteristics of a Traditional Japanese Approach to Learning. In *Learning in Likely Places*, ed. J. Singleton, 68–84. New York: Cambridge University Press.

Doi, T. (1973). *The Anatomy of Dependence.* Tokyo: Kodansha International.

Eisenberg, N. (1992). *The Caring Child.* Cambridge, MA: Harvard University Press.

Eisenberg, N., & Spinrad, T. (2004). Emotion-Related Regulation: Sharpening the Definition. *Child Development* 75 (2): 334–39.

Embree, J. F. (1939). *Suye Mura: A Japanese Village.* Chicago: University of Chicago Press.

Feiman-Nemser, S., & Floden, R. (1986). The Cultures of Teaching. In *Handbook of Research on Teaching*, ed. M. Wittrock, 505–26. 3ʳᵈ ed. New York: Macmillan.

Feiman-Nemser, S. (2001). From Preparation to Practice: Designing a Continuum to Strengthen and Sustain Teaching. *Teacher College Record* 103: 1013–55.

Foucault, M. (1977). *Discipline and Punish: The Birth of the Prison.* New York: Random House.

Friedkin, Shelley. (1999). What Is Lesson Study? http://www.lessonresearch.net.

Fukuzawa, R. E., & LeTendre, G. (2001). *Intense Years: How Japanese Adolescents Balance School, Family, and Friends.* New York: RoutledgeFalmer.

Gaskins, S., & Paradise, R. (2009). Learning through Observation in Daily Life. In *The Anthropology of Learning in Childhood*, ed. D. F. Lancy, J. Bock, & S. Gaskins, 85–117. Lanham, MD: AltaMira Press.

Goffman, E. (1971). *Relations in Public: Microstudies of the Public Order.* New York: Harper & Row.

Grossman, D. (2009). *On Killing: The Psychological Cost of Learning to Kill in War and Society.* New York: Back Bay Books.

Hayashi, A. (2011). The Japanese Hands-Off Approach to Curriculum Guidelines for Early Childhood Education as a Form of Cultural Practice. *Asian-Pacific Journal of Research in Early Childhood Education* 5 (2): 107–23.

Hayashi, A., Karasawa, M., & Tobin, J. (2009). The Japanese Preschool's Pedagogy of Feeling: Cultural Strategies for Supporting Young Children's Emotional Development. *Ethos* 37 (1): 32–49.

Hayashi, A., & Tobin, J. (2011). The Japanese Preschool's Pedagogy of Peripheral Participation. *Ethos* 39 (2): 139–64.

Hayashi, A., & Tobin, J. (2012). Reframing a Visual Ethnography of a Japanese Preschool Classroom. *Visual Anthropology Review* 28 (1): 13–31.

Hayashi, A., & Tobin, J. (2014). The Power of Implicit Teaching Practices: Continuities and Discontinuities in Pedagogical Approaches of Deaf and Hearing Preschools in Japan. *Comparative Education Review* 58 (1): 24–46.

Hess, R., Azuma, H., Kashiwagi, K., Dickson, P., Nagano, S., Holloway, S., Miyake, K., Price, G., Hatano, G., & McDevitt, T. (1986). Family Influences on School Readiness and Achievement in Japan and the United States: An Overview of a Longitudinal Study. In *Child Development and Education in Japan*, ed. H. Stevenson, H. Azuma, & K. Hakuta. New York: W. H. Freeman.

Hindmarsh, J., & Pilnick, A. (2007). Knowing Bodies at Work: Embodiment and Ephemeral Teamwork in Anaesthesia. *Organization Studies* 28 (9): 1395–1416.

Hoffman, D. (1995). Models of Self and Culture in Teaching and Learning: An Anthropological Perspective on Japanese and American Education. *Educational Foundations* 9 (3): 19–42.

Hoffman, D. (2000). Pedagogies of Self in American and Japanese Early Childhood Education: A Critical Conceptual Analysis. *Elementary School Journal* 101 (2): 193–208.

Holloway, S. (2000). *Contested Childhood: Diversity and Change in Japanese Preschools*. London, UK: Routledge.

Hubbard, J. (2008). Misc. Notes on the Kawabata and Oe readings. http://sophia.smith.edu/~jhubbard/syllabi/ContempJapan/kawabata.htm, accessed July 17.

Hutchins, E., & Klausen, T. (1996). Distributed Cognition in an Airline Cockpit. In *Cognition and Communication at Work*, ed. Y. Engestrom & D. Middleton, 15–34. New York: Cambridge University Press.

Ishigaki, E. (1999). New Perspectives of Early Childhood Teacher Education in Japan: Concerning New Revisions of Guidelines and the Juvenile Welfare Law. *Educare* 20: 21–34.

Jackson, S. (1996). Toward a Conceptual Understanding of the Flow Experience in Elite Athletes. *Research Quarterly for Exercise and Sport* 67 (1): 76–90.

Juniper, A. (2003). *Wabi Sabi: The Japanese Art of Impermanence*. North Clarendon, VT: Tuttle.

Klinger, D. (2006). *Into the Kill Zone: A Cop's View of Deadly Force*. San Francisco: Jossey Bass.

Kojima, H. (1986). Child Rearing Concepts as a Belief System of the Society and the Individual. In *Child Development and Education in Japan*, ed. H. Stevenson, H. Azuma, & K. Hakuta, 39–54. New York: Freeman.

Koren, L. (1994). *Wabi-Sabi: For Artists, Designers, Poets and Philosophers*. Berkeley: Stone Bridge.

Latour, B. (2005). *Reassembling the Social: An Introduction to Actor-Network-Theory*. Oxford: Oxford University Press.

Lave, J., & Wenger, E. (1991). *Situated Learning: Legitimate Peripheral Participation*. Cambridge: Cambridge University Press.

Lebra, T. (1976). *Japanese Patterns of Behavior*. Honolulu: University of Hawaii Press.

LeTendre, G. (2000). *Learning to Be Adolescent: Growing Up in US and Japanese Middle Schools*. New Haven: Yale University Press.

Lewis, C. (1984). Cooperation and Control in Japanese Nursery Schools. *Comparative Education Review* 28 (1): 69–84.

Lewis, C. (1995). *Educating Hearts and Minds: Reflections on Japanese Preschool and Elementary Education*. Cambridge: Cambridge University Press.

Lewis, C. (2009). What Is the Nature of Knowledge Development in Lesson Study? *Education Action Research* 17 (1): 95–110.

Lewis, C., Perry, R., & Murata, A. (2006). How Should Research Contribute to Instructional Improvement? The Case of Lesson Study. *Educational Researcher* 35 (3): 3–14.

Loughran, J. J. (2007). Science Teacher as Learner. *Handbook of Research on Science Education*, 1043–65.

Lutz, C. (1988). *Unnatural Emotions: Everyday Sentiments on a Micronesian Atoll and Their Challenge to Western Theory*. Chicago: University of Chicago Press.

Maret, J. (2008). An Ethnography of Invisibility: Education and Special Need Children in Japan. PhD Diss., University of Hawaii.

Markus, H. R., & Kitayama, S. (1991). Culture and the Self: Implications for Cognition, Emotion, and Motivation. *Psychological Review* 98: 224–53.

Mauss, M. (1934/1973). Techniques of the Body. *Economy and Society* 2 (1): 70–88.

Merleau-Ponty, M. (1964). *The Visible and the Invisible*. Trans. A. Lingis. Evanston, IL: Northwestern University Press.

Ministry of Education, Culture, Sports, Science, and Technology (MEXT). (2008). *Yōchien Kyōiku Yōryō* (The Course of Study about Early Childhood Education and Care).

Ministry of Education, Culture, Sports, Science, and Technology (MEXT). (2009). *Yōji Kyōiku Jitsutai Chōsa* (The Survey of Early Childhood Education).

Morita, Y., & Kiyonaga, K. (1996). *Bullying—Pathology in Classroom*. Tokyo: Kaneko Shobo.

Nakamura, K. (2006). *Deaf in Japan: Signing and Politics of Identity*. Ithaca, NY: Cornell University Press.

Nakatsubo, F., Minowa, J., Akita, K., Sunagami, F., Yasumi, K., & Masuda, T. (2009). A Study of the Involvement of Japanese Early Childhood Teachers in Clean-up Time. *Asia-Pacific Journal of Research in Early Childhood Education* 3 (1): 69–85.

Oda, Y., & Mori, M. (2006). Current Challenges of Kindergarten (*Yōchien*) Education in Japan: Toward Balancing Children's Autonomy and Teachers' Intention. *Childhood Education* 82 (6): 369–73.

Olson, S., Kashiwagi, K., & Crystal, D. (2001). Concepts of Adaptive and Maladaptive Child Behavior: A Comparison of U.S. and Japanese Mothers of Preschool-Age Children. *Journal of Cross-Cultural Psychology* 32 (1): 43–57.

Paine, L. (1990). The Teachers as Virtuoso: A Chinese Model for Teaching. *Teachers College Record* 92 (1): 49–81.

Paine, L., & Fang, Y. (2007). Dilemmas in Reforming China's Teachers: Assuring "Quality" in Professional Development. In *Reforming Teaching Globally*, ed. M. T. Tatto. Oxford: Symposium Books.

Peak, L. (1991). *Learning to Go to School in Japan: The transition from Home to Preschool Life*. Berkeley: University of California Press.

Polanyi, M. (1962). Tacit Knowing: Its Bearing on Some Problems of Philosophy. *Reviews of Modern Physics* 34 (4): 601–15.

Polanyi, M. (1966). *The Tacit Dimension*. Chicago: University of Chicago Press.

Raeff, C. (2000). European-American Parents' Ideas about Their Toddlers' Independence and Interdependence. *Journal of Applied Developmental Psychology* 21 (2): 183–205.

Raeff, C. (2006). Individuals in Relation to Others: Independence and Interdependence in a Kindergarten Classroom. *Ethos* 34 (4): 521–57.

Rogoff, B., Paradise, R., Arauz, M. R., Correa-Chavez, M., & Angelillo, C. (2003). First Hand Learning through Intent Participation. *Annual Review of Psychology* 54: 175–203.

Rohlen, T. P. (1974). *For Harmony and Strength: Japanese White-Collar Organization in Anthropological Perspective*. Berkeley: University of California Press.

Rosenberger, N. R. (1989). Dialectic Balance in the Polar Model of Self: The Japan Case. *Ethos* 17 (1): 88–113.

Sato, M., Chung Wei, R., & Darling-Hammond, L. (2008). Improving Teachers' Assessment Practices through Professional Development: The Case of National Board Certification. *American Educational Research Journal* 45 (3): 669–700.

Sato, N. E. (2004). *Inside Japanese Classrooms*. New York: RoutledgeFalmer.

Schempp, P., Tan, S., Manross, D., & Fincher, M. (1998). Differences in Novice and Competent Teachers' Knowledge. *Teachers and Teaching: Theory and Practice* 4 (1): 9–20.

Sharp, R., & Green, A. (1975). *Education and Social Control*. London: Routledge & Kegan Paul.

Shimizu, H. (2000). Japanese Cultural Psychology and Empathic Understanding: Implications for Academic and Cultural Psychology. *Ethos* 28 (2): 224–47.

Singleton, J., ed. (1998). *Learning in Likely Places*. New York: Cambridge University Press.

Smith, R. J., & Wiswell, E. L. (1982). *The Women of Suye Mura*. Chicago: University of Chicago Press.

Spiro, R. J., Collins, B. P., & Ramchandran, A. R. (2007). Modes of Openness and Flexibility in Cognitive Flexibility Hypertext Learning Environments. In *Flexible Learning in an Information Society*, ed. B. Khan, 18–25. Hershey, PA: Information Science Publishing.

Spiro, R. J., Feltovich, P., Jacobson, M. J., & Coulson, R. L. (1992). Cognitive Flexibility, Constructivism, and Hypertext: Random Access Instruction for Advanced Knowledge Acquisition in Ill-Structured Domains. In *Constructivism and the Technology of Instruction*, ed. T. Duffy & D. Jonassen, 57–76. Hillsdale, NJ: Erlbaum.

Stigler, J. W., & Hiebert, J. (1999). *The Teaching Gap: Best Ideas from the World's Teachers for Improving Education in the Classroom*. New York: Free Press.

Stokoe, W. C. (1980). *Sign and Culture*. Silver Spring, MD: Linstok Press.

Titchener, E. (1909). Experimental Psychology of the Thought Processes. New York: Macmillan.

Tobin, J., Hsueh, Y., & Karasawa, M. (2009). *Preschool in Three Cultures Revisited: China, Japan, and the United States*. Chicago: University of Chicago Press.

Tobin, J., Wu, D., & Davidson, D. (1987). Class Size and Student/Teacher Ratios. *Comparative Education Review* 31 (4): 533–49.

Tobin, J., Wu, D., & Davidson, D. (1989). *Preschool in Three Cultures: Japan, China and the United States*. New Haven: Yale University Press.

Walsh, D. (2002). The Development of Self in Japanese Preschools: Negotiating Space. In *Research in International Education: Experience, Theory, and Practice*, ed. L. Bresler & A. Ardichvili, 213–46. New York: Peter Lang.

Walsh, D. J. (2004). Frog Boy and the American Monkey: The Body in Japanese Early Schooling. In *Knowing Bodies, Moving Minds*, ed. L. Bresler, 97–109. Dordrecht: Kluwer Academic Publishers.

White, J. J. (1989). Student Teaching as a Rite of Passage. *Anthropology and Education Quarterly* 20 (3): 177–95.

White, M., & LeVine, R. (1986). What Is an *Ii Ko* (Good Child)? In *Child Development and Education in Japan*, ed. H. Stevenson, H. Azuma, & K. Hakuta, 55–62. New York: W. H. Freeman.

Valente, J. M. (2010). *d/Deaf and d/Dumb: A Portrait of a Deaf Kid as a Young Superhero*. Disability Studies in Education 6. New York: Peter Lang.

van Manen, M. (1995). On the Epistemology of Reflective Practice. *Teachers and Teaching: Theory and Practice* 1 (1): 33–50.

Zeichner, K. M., & Gore, J. (1990). Teacher Socialization. In *Handbook of research on teacher education*, ed. W. R. Houston, 329–48. New York: Macmillan.

Index

Abu-Lughod, Lila, 70
actor network theory (ANT), 156–57, 158
ajito (hideaways), 30–32
Akiba, Motoko, 73–74
Akita, Kiyomi, 139–40
Althusser, Louis, 6
amae, 17, 41–44; development of teachers' expertise about, 117–19; English translation of, 43; loneliness and, 43–44, 46, 55; *mimamoru* and, 37–38; *omoiyari* and, 44, 45, 55; as relational emotion, 55
Anatomy of Dependence, The (Doi), 42–43
Anderson-Levitt, Katherine, 2–3
anthropology, nonjudgmental cultural relativism in, 114–15. *See also* ethnography; psychological anthropology
apology: bowing to indicate, 81–82, 89, 93–96; flow of bodies in space and, 104; hairpulling fight and, 50, 91–93, 95; tug-of-war fight and, 27
apprenticeship learning, 69, 110, 124, 126–28, 129, 133
architecture of Japanese preschools: development of teachers and, 133–34; *kejime* and, 86; *mimamoru* and, 30–32, 166; official guidelines for, 142; teddy bear fight and, 157, 166
Art and Answerability (Bakhtin), 38
Asch, Patsy, 15
Asch, Timothy, 15
attention: by children responding to child's loneliness, 46; *mimamoru* as performance of, 24; of teachers in public deaf programs, 148; teacher's performance of, 7, 9, 24–25, 30
authoritative bodily techniques, 83
Azuma, Hiroshi, 114

Bakhtin, Mikhail, 38, 82–83, 98
Bandura, Albert, 69
Ben-Ari, Eyal, 53, 70, 87
Bentham, Jeremy, 77
Berliner, David, 10, 109–10, 113, 122
Bloch, Maurice, 8, 14, 121–22, 130–31, 158, 159
bodily citationality, 82–83, 97–101
bodily techniques, 3, 4–5, 159–60; authorita-

tive, 90–91, 96; Bakhtinian analysis of, 82–83; characteristically Japanese, 82, 104–5; contexts of, 83–87; in doing *mimamoru*, 23–24; internally persuasive, 83; of Japanese children, 82–87, 168–69; learned through experience, 9; Mauss on, 4, 23–24, 159; pedagogies of, 85–89; of students imitating teachers, 83, 97–101; synchronization of bodies in, 11–12; tacit nature of, 9; teachers' talk about, 6. *See also* bowing; embodied practice; intercorporeality
body and mind, 5, 6, 159, 160
bōkansha (bystander), 67
Bourdieu, Pierre, 6–7, 10, 156, 159, 160–61
bowing, 89–93; as attempted apology, 81–82, 93–96; contexts of, 84, 87–92; in different registers of formality, 90–92, 171; hybrid forms of, 93–96; before meals, 87, 91, 97
bullying (*ijime*), 73–75
busyness of teacher: fights/disputes of children and, 10, 28–30, 166–67; juggling competing demands, 170; in public deaf programs, 148–49

child-centered philosophy, 139
child development, Western vs. Japanese concepts of, 71–73, 76–77
childlikeness (*kodomo-rashii*), 43, 144, 145
citationality, bodily, 82–83, 97–101
Clark, Scott, 105
collective self-regulation, 71–73, 75, 77
Collins, B. P., 11, 114
Connor, Linda, 15
context, 83–87; of bowing, 84, 87–92; contingency and, 11; empty-mindedness and, 114, 115; negotiating space and, 103; shifts from informal to formal registers according to, 12, 17; teacher's practice emerging from, 170. *See also kejime*
contingency, 10–11, 114, 157, 165, 170
co-sleeping, 53, 54, 70, 102
Coulson, R. L., 11
Crossley, Nick, 5
cultural explanations of teaching, 2–4, 6, 23, 156–57, 165, 170–71
culture. *See* Japanese culture